Inside Magazines
A Career Builder's Guide

T0347747

Also by Michael Barnard

MAGAZINE AND JOURNAL PRODUCTION
INTRODUCTION TO PRINT BUYING
MAKING ELECTRONIC MANUSCRIPTS
THE PRINT AND PRODUCTION MANUAL (WITH PEACOCK, BERRILL)
THE POCKET GLOSSARY OF ADVERTISING TERMS
THE POCKET GLOSSARY OF PRINTING, BINDING AND PAPER TERMS
THE POCKET GLOSSARY OF DESIGN AND TYPOGRAPHIC TERMS
THE PUBLISHER'S GUIDE TO DESKTOP PUBLISHING (WITH WILSON-DAVIES, ST. JOHN BATE)

Inside Magazines
A Career Builder's Guide

Michael Barnard

Routledge
Taylor & Francis Group

LONDON AND NEW YORK

Published in the United Kingdom by
Blueprint Publishing Ltd
in association with
The Periodical Publishers Association
First published 1989
Reprinted 2004
by Routledge,
11 New Fetter Lane, London EC4P 4EE

Transferred to Digital Printing 2004

British Library Cataloguing in Publication Data

Barnard, Michael 1944-
    Inside magazines: a career builder's guide
    1. Great Britain. Magazine publishing industries
    I. Title
    338.4'7070572'0941

    Hardback ISBN 0 948905 44 1
    Paperback ISBN 0 948905 36 0

Typeset from wordprocessor files by Macmillan Production Ltd, Little Essex Street, London WC2R 3LF

Contents

Acknowledgements

People who work in magazine publishing have many demands on their time. I am genuinely grateful that so many spared so much of theirs to help me with this book. It is impossible to list all those who gave advice but I would particularly like to thank the following, whose time I took up in copious quantities: David Arculus of EMAP, Simon Taylor of Haymarket Publishing, Ray Barker of Macmillan Magazines, David Hall of Haymarket Publishing, Keith Lane of Quadrant Publishing Services, Ian Locks of The Periodical Publishers Association, Ron Sumption of The Periodicals Training Council and Rebecca Singer of Macmillan. Many thanks too to Blueprint Publishing for permission to use extracts from *Magazine and Journal Production*.

Introduction

THIS BOOK is an attempt to describe the nature of the jobs in a magazine publishing company to enable the potential employee to form a view on whether this type of career will suit him.

So there is no misunderstanding, let me nail my colours firmly to the mast: I think working in magazine publishing is great. It's fun, it's creative and it can be financially rewarding.

But at the same time let's be realistic: it's demanding, it's competitive and it's unforgiving. It's a career for people with lively minds and mental and physical stamina.

In periodical publishing, nothing succeeds like success.

If you want a quiet life, read no further. In the company I work for there are people around in the publishing offices from 8am until well after the pubs open in the evening (contrary to popular belief) and often at weekends and on public holidays too. Of course, they don't all work from 8am until 9pm seven days a week but the nine-to-five routine is unknown here. And we're no different from any other magazine publisher. The press deadline is a hard taskmaster and it rules everyone in the organisation.

The people who work on periodicals are enthusiasts and they are demanding of themselves and their colleagues. So add to the list of desirable qualities a resilience to people-pressure.

In this book, in addition to identifying specific jobs, I've tried to describe how this ethos affects the various disciplines involved in the magazine publishing industry. Talents vary, of course, and it is unlikely that the advertising salesman and the graphic designer have the same skills, but to work successfully in this business they do need to share something of the same personal qualities.

In chapter ten I say:

> Most magazine publishers have only two principal assets: their magazines and their staff. Unlike a manufacturing industry, there are no machines which can make or break the company; there is no succession of really dramatic new technologies which will change the nature of the business year by year. The company will succeed or fail depending on the skills of the staff in putting together magazines which the readers want to read and the advertisers want to use.

In other words, this business is about people.

This book is consequently written with an eye on how individuals might or might not be suited to the jobs described and it is clearly therefore something of a personal view. The Periodical Publishers Association, which represents the magazine industry in the UK, has been kind enough to support my efforts because it believes such an introduction is much needed but it would be unfair of me to involve them in all my prejudices and I should point out that the views expressed here are not necessarily those of the PPA.

I have many thanks to give to those who have helped me put together this book and I have noted these separately because, to use advertising jargon, they deserve a solus position.

But I also have one apology to make: my journalistic skills have not been up to the task of ensuring I have fairly allocated 'hes' and 'shes' when writing about magazine staff and against the current fashion I have stuck to the male gender. This is also against the evidence, for magazine publishing is generously staffed with women in all departments and at all levels and I would not want my apparent male chauvinism to be construed as anything other than literary inadequacy.

The publishers, the PPA and I believe there will be future editions of this book so any comments will be gratefully received.

MB

'. . . launches of more modest product carried out with the proceeds of a second mortgage on the family home, the scrapings from the bottom of the building society account and a wish and a prayer.'

1
The Periodical
Publishing Scene

THE PERIODICAL PRESS is prolific and diverse, expanding and profitable.

The industry, which is concentrated fairly heavily in the south of England, comprises an amazingly wide variety of titles, ranging from journals covering arcane specialisms and selling only a few hundred copies to consumer magazines with circulations of over one million.

This plethora of publications provides about 20,000 jobs. And this figure is unlikely to fall. In a recent manpower survey commissioned by the Periodicals Training Council only 1% of companies interviewed expected to be employing fewer staff in the future.

Equally encouragingly for those comtemplating careers in magazines, the same survey showed 44% of companies reporting current manpower shortages.

Not only are the periodicals themselves disparate but so also are the organisations which own them. Anyone can start or own a magazine.

In recent years there have been many mergers and takeovers resulting in ever-larger and more powerful corporations with extensive lists of titles. But economy of scale is not necessarily a feature of all types of periodical publishing and alongside the titles published by the giant multi-nationals there also appear thousands of publications issued by small companies, learned societies, professional organisations and individuals, although it is interesting to note that over half the industry's total workforce is employed by the 10 biggest companies.

The cost of launching a mass-circulation consumer magazine is such that only those with access to substantial resources can join the game, but there are many other launches of more modest product carried out with the proceeds of a second mortgage on the family home, the scrapings from the bottom of the building society account and a wish and a prayer.

Either type of endeavour is vulnerable to the vagaries of the marketplace and may fail; equally, of course, either can gain a toehold and in due course create kudos and riches for its proprietors.

There have been many launches, both big and small, in recent years, adding to the size and variety of the industry. In 1988 about 7% of the total magazine market was represented by new launches. The numbers of new titles and the reasonable success rates achieved are fair indicators of the health of the industry.

Industry size

It is difficult to put an accurate figure on the number of magazines published in the UK due to a largely semantic but nonetheless lively debate about what qualifies a magazine to be so named.

To side-step any 'misnomer' charges and still take a top-end figure we can safely say that there are about 10,000 'periodical titles' published in the UK, including academic journals and directories but excluding newspapers.

Benn's *Media Directory* analyses them into 386 classifications (by subject) but this is not a particularly helpful division for our purposes.

There are various methods of classification we could use

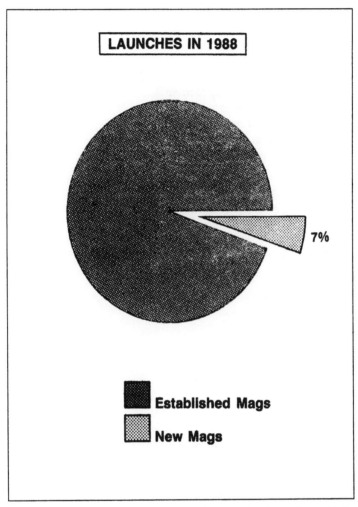

Fig 1. There have been many launches, both big and small, in recent years, adding to the size and variety of the industry. In 1988 about 7% of the total magazine market was represented by new launches. (Illustration courtesy of the Periodical Publishers Association.)

but for simplicity's sake I propose the following rather arbitrary breakdown:

Consumer publications

Newspaper colour supplements
Women's magazines
General interest magazines
Special interest magazines
Programme magazines

Business publications

News publications

News magazines
Newsletters

Academic journals

Society-owned
Publisher-owned

House magazines

Various sub-divisions could be identified in some detail. For example, we could divide women's magazines into:

Weeklies
Young women's weeklies
Monthlies
Home interest
Health, beauty, fitness
Child care
Romance

... and business magazines may be divided into almost as many sub-categories. But to consider the implications for career development our simplistic approach is adequate. Let's look briefly at the characteristics of each group.

Consumer publications

This mass-market section of the periodical press more than any other is visibly dependent on the flair of those who work in it and the changing economic and social patterns in the marketplace. In this respect it is sometimes a more volatile sector.

If a man needs the information contained in the periodical which serves his business or profession, he will be slow to cancel his order even though the editorial team are clearly crass idiots and the journal looks like a dog's dinner. Similarly, the advertisers will use the medium if it continues to get to the readers they wish to reach. The publication will in due course be overtaken by a competitor and probably die of inertia but this can take a little time and meanwhile opportunities arise for reform.

The mass-market consumer magazine is more immediately at the mercy of the fickle reader's passing fancies about how to spend his disposable income. And because the reader's fancies pass, so must the formulae which produce successful consumer magazines. They must change and evolve, lead and respond to fashion, style and social change.

Newspaper colour supplements are really in a slightly different category from the paid-for consumer magazines since their distribution depends on the success of their parent newspaper. Similarly free-distribution magazines are not dependent on copy sales for their health and wealth. But in either case, an uninteresting or irrelevant magazine will not succeed because the advertisers will not use it.

The shape of the consumer press has changed significantly in the last couple of decades. Newspaper colour magazines have become almost universal; there has been a dramatic smartening up of the women's magazines and many new up-market launches; programme magazines (like *Time Out* in London) have invented successful new formulae for providing readers with this sort of information; and it would be fair to claim that much imagination has been applied to content, presentation and marketing.

After some periods of rather desultory publishing, the consumer press is enjoying a boom. In 1988 it enjoyed a 24% advertising growth rate, compared with television at 14% and the national press at 15%.

An interesting new phenomenon is the entrance of European publishers into the UK consumer magazine marketplace, especially with women's magazines. Gruner & Jahr, the magazine subsidiary of the German publisher, Bertlesmann, launched Prima to much acclaim and this has been followed by other European invasions, with the UK consumer publishers fighting back imaginatively. The result has been a healthy growth in the size of the market.

Most consumer magazines are either weeklies or monthlies.

Business publications

Business and professional publications represent the most prolific sector of the periodical press. Their range, both in content and presentation, is wide, with black-and-white tabloid, newspaper-type product often competing in the same market as highly-designed, glossy magazines stuffed with four-colour advertisements.

Over 3,000 are published at frequencies ranging from weekly to quarterly.

The editorial content is specific and sometimes technical and many of the journalists are drawn from the business sectors covered by the publications. But again there is a wide variation: journals which are esoteric and unintelligible to the general public are sold alongside those which are editorially accessible to any interested reader.

Many are powerful instruments within the communities they serve and are often the catalysts for change within a business or profession. The general press relies heavily on them for its business and professional information. Often they are newsworthy themselves, leading campaigns for change or commenting with authority on topical subjects. Magazines serving employees in the National Health Service, for example, have been widely quoted and consulted as the great NHS debate rolls on.

In recent years, their quality and the professionalism of their staff have improved dramatically. Much good journalism, design and sales and marketing expertise is now clearly visible.

The style of such magazines is often influenced by the need to carry topical news and tightly scheduled recruitment advertising, creating a working environment sometimes closer to a newspaper than a consumer magazine, with late deadlines and considerable editorial, production and advertisement sales pressure, especially in the weeklies. As a medium for both editorial and advertising they have never been more successful. In 1988 ad revenues in this sector were up by 25%, according to the Advertising Association.

From the all-media total for 'business-to-business' advertising, the business press takes about 35%, compared with brochures and catalogues at 15%, newspapers at 8% and TV at less than 2%.

News publications

News magazines like *The Economist* present some of the finest and most authoritative contemporary journalism and of necessity have highly efficient sales, production and distribution systems. There are only a handful of English language news magazines but they are as big and powerful as the world's great newspapers and their influence is international. *The Economist, Time,* and *Newsweek* are read throughout the world and employ large numbers of highly professional staff.

They are all weeklies.

Newsletters are arguably more properly considered with the professional press, but I have included them here to avoid semantic confusion.

This type of medium has increased hugely in popularity in recent years and is now a thriving sector. Most newsletters are simply presented (sometimes even wordprocessed) with small, closely-targeted circulations. The emphasis is entirely on the quality of the information carried, in terms either of its topicality or explicit relevance to the specialist reader.

Typically they do not carry advertising and have expensive subscriptions. There are daily, weekly and monthly examples. They have small staffs but are often highly authoritative in specialist areas and frequently organise conferences and seminars which back up what is essentially an information service.

Academic journals

Academic or 'learned' journals are the publcations in which academic papers and the results of original research are published. A learned journal can be owned by a learned society and published by a professional publisher, owned and published by a society, or owned and published by a publishing company.

Most of the editorial content is submitted by academics and no payment is made although there may be a limited amount of professionally written material.

Some publishers of learned journals have full-time publishing staff committed to editorial, production and circulation work on these publications but often they are put together by an out-house editor who selects and rejects manuscripts with the help of an editorial board. In these circumstances the publisher may arrange production and circulation and handle the business administration.

There is a trend towards carrying advertising in academic journals, although this is still far from general. Many are monthly or quarterly and some appear, by design or accident, less frequently.

Often the editorial policy is dictated by an editorial board appointed by the learned society the journal represents.

House magazines

House magazines is the generic term for newsletters, journals or magazines published by companies or other organisations for internal consumption.

There are many thousands of house magazines in the UK. They range from modest in the extreme – photocopied, typewritten newssheets – to a lavishness which knows no bounds of economic restraint. Similarly, the staffing arrangements for house mags embrace the enthusiastic part-timer and the highly professional team of journalists, photographers and designers.

Their purpose may be simply to communicate facts and figures, to keep one part of a company in touch with another, or to present a prestigious face and maintain a selected profile of an organisation and its place in the world.

At the highest level, polished standards of journalism, design and production are exhibited and some rewarding and influential jobs are available.

Editors of house magazines have their own organisation, the British Association of Industrial Editors (which naturally has its own house magazine!).

The career path here can be mapped differently from the trail leading through mainstream magazine publishing; we touch on it again in chapter two: The Way In.

The future

Television has been the most significant competitor for advertising revenue – the lifeblood of many magazines – since commercial TV first started, but in recent years there have been indications that the magazine press is more than holding its own after some disappointing losses of market share in the early eighties.

The Advertising Association tells us that magazine ad revenues finished 1988 just short of £1bn (including production costs) and we have noted that this represents a healthy growth in both consumer and business sectors. Total circulation also rose during the year, according to a report on the magazine market commissioned by the Periodical Publishers Association (PPA), the leading industry body.

We have also seen that new launches accounted for about 7% of the total market and, as the PPA comments in its report: 'The ratio of successful to unsuccessful launches is quite heavily weighted on the successful side. This indicates that the market for magazines has by no means reached saturation point. There is still considerable demand for magazines and periodicals, and ample niche space for them to launch into.'

Profitability

In terms of profitability the trade performs well, having turned in a respectable average 10.5% pre-tax profit on sales in the last year for which figures are available (1986/7).

Economically, therefore, the industry presents an encouraging image. As a career option it has further attractions.

Standards of professionalism within the industry are increasing rapidly and training, as we shall see in a later chapter, is becoming formalised and structured. The impact of technology, too, is being felt in all disciplines within the trade. Many outmoded and unproductive practices are being changed on the production side of the business and computerisation goes on apace within the office environment and the circulation areas.

The periodical press is looking healthy and progressive, offering some excellent career opportunities within a lively if demanding industry.

'Some perseverence may be required.'

2
The Way In

IT IS NOT particularly difficult for an intelligent, energetic person to get a job on a magazine. As we've seen, periodical publishing is an expanding industry and recruitment is a constant process. But as with all trades where personal qualities are important, some perseverence may be required.

In the following chapters we look at specific jobs and comment on the demands made on the individuals who choose those careers. Here we will take a broad look at entry routes into those areas.

Editorial

There are no nationally recognised vocational qualifications for magazine journalists although this seems likely to change in due course (see chapter 11: Training), so the way into the industry on the editorial side is less clearly defined than in many other trades or professions.

This is particularly true in the business press where experts in a business subject who happen to have some journalistic talent are as likely to be employed as journalists with knowledge specific to a business.

Many journalists working on magazines started professional

life as newspaper reporters or in some other sector of the media. For those with no previous full-time professional experience, three points are worth noting:

1. Good academic qualifications are becoming increasingly important. More than 80% of all newcomers to magazine journalism have been educated up to at least A-level standard and many have degrees.
2. It is a good idea for the applicant previously to have tried his hand at writing, in however humble a capacity. School and university magazines, contributions to the local paper, pieces for the parish magazine ... all can help to demonstrate that the newcomer wants to write and can write.
3. There are pre-entry courses available (see Chapter 11 on Training) and there is no doubt that such training is valuable in itself and provides an indication of seriousness about a career.

The relevance of academic qualifications is a favourite debate among journalists, with some old-timers who could hardly string together a couple of O-level GCEs hotly contesting the relevance of a first-class honours degree in classics to an editorial job on the *Bricklayer's Quarterly*.

Certainly it is possible to point to many eminent journalists whose formal education did not proceed beyond secondary level. But the matter is really purely pragmatic: editors like to employ intelligent staff and the conventional method of assessing the application of intelligence among young people is, rightly or wrongly, academic qualification. Until such time as a vocational qualification exists, this is likely to be one of the first criteria.

The need to demonstrate embryonic writing skills is less contentious. Ron Sumption, head of the Periodicals Training Council, strongly recommends some form of previous writing experience to all those who contact the PTC asking about entry to magazine journalism. 'We always tell them they should be able to produce something they've written if they have no previous professional experience as a journalist,' he states.

Pre-entry courses are referred to in greater detail in chapter 11 (Training). In a report on *Manpower and Training in the Periodical Publishing Industry* commissioned by the PPA and the PTC, most employers expressed themselves satisfied with the quality of staff coming off such courses.

Applying for jobs

The methods of application for jobs in the industry are fairly conventional.

Newcomers can write to companies of course and this is how many journalists got their first jobs. Towards the end of this book there is a list of the names and addresses of all the members of the Periodical Publishers Association (representing about 80% of the industry, if measured by revenue).

Jobs are advertised. *The Guardian* Media section carries many vacancies each week. So do the trade magazines, *UK Press Gazette, Magazine Week* and *The Publisher*.

Some newcomers begin with non-editorial jobs (for example, secretarial) and move across when opportunities occur.

Some aspiring magazine journalists decide to go through the mill on a local newspaper first – not a bad idea for those who want to be sure of a wide experience.

Good magazine journalists need many qualities of which the most important is probably common sense. The ability to write clear, concise English is of course essential. In the business press it is often necessary to have a facility for the analysis of masses of information which needs to be presented clearly and compactly to the reader.

And, for all magazine staff, stamina is necessary. The show never closes and long hours and sustained pressure are common features of the working life.

Advertisement sales

On the advertising side, many sales people joined up with their magazines in response to advertisements (of course!) and were trained on the job. Here academic qualifications are possibly less critical although an increasing number of senior advertising staff have university educations.

Generally speaking, getting a job in a magazine advertisement department should not be difficult if the candidate is right for it. If he can't sell himself, he probably can't sell advertisement space!

The qualities necessary are those required of any salesperson – optimism, self-assurance and tenacity – together with enough discipline to ensure that the paperwork gets processed.

In the survey mentioned above, most companies reported shortages of good advertisement sales staff, so job opportunities are certainly available.

Design

In design, the way in is normally through a graphic design qualification. Nearly all art colleges offer graphic design courses to varying levels, up to degree standard.

As with journalists, evidence of your work is necessary. The designer who applies for a job with a portfolio of impressive samples (albeit only straight from art college) is more likely to get a place than the contender who relies on theoretical qualifications alone.

It is particularly important that a designer working in a magazine environment has acquired a good working knowledge of print production processes. There is little time to re-think ideas which turn out to be technically impracticable and the designer whose work will not translate into cost-effective production is one of the magazine production manager's least favourite colleagues. Designers on magazines need to be talented (of course), quick and calm.

House magazines

The ways in to jobs on house magazines are somewhat different from the straight magazine publishing routes.

House magazine staff may be professional journalists, in which case they are taken on board after a spell on newspapers or magazines in the 'outside world', and will typically apply in response to advertisements in the trade press or hear of jobs on the grapevine. But often staff are recruited from within the journal's parent organisation – maybe from the press office, the public relations department or a marketing division.

Many companies sub-contract the putting together of their house magazines to independent editorial and production units. These tend to be staffed by quite experienced professionals who have a solid career background on magazines or newspapers.

There are few house magazines which can support extensive training for new staff so there is much to be said for external experience before commitment to an internal publication. However, some such publications – especially those put out by multi-national companies with large internal resources – are quite impressive productions and can offer good career prospects.

It should go without saying that anyone planning to work on a house magazine should essentially be in sympathy with the activities and policies of the organisation it represents. The anti-smoking campaigner will not find a suitable platform for his journalistic conscience in the house magazine of a tobacco company.

Graduate schemes

Some of the larger publishing companies have particular schemes for the recruitment and development of graduates they believe will become high fliers in due course. Some visit the universities or mail the college careers advisors.

The schemes vary from company to company. We discuss these further in chapter 11.

Salaries

Salaries are of course of abiding interest to everyone both in terms of subsistence in one's early working life and as a measure of potential prosperity as careers develop.

As with many trades and professions, the early days in a publishing career can be hard going. Most publishing companies would claim to be meritocratic, with the result that starting salaries are relatively modest, in line with the contribution the newcomer can make to the business, but escalate fairly quickly as experience and skill acquire an increased value.

Basic salary grades related to job titles are common in many publishing houses, whether agreed with a trade union or established independently, but it is not unusual for the more talented staff to be paid above these grades. Trainees are often taken on with salaries fixed at a percentage of the basic grade during the period of 'apprenticeship'. This might typically be 80 or 90%.

It is difficult to be at all specific since there are no national agreements covering publishing salaries but it is fair to say that starting salaries tend to be pitched against those of other industries competing for similar levels of trainee.

It is interesting to note that a company's starting level does not appear to bear any fixed relationship to its general level of salaries for experienced staff, so it could be inferred that a high starting salary when offered may only be a short-term advantage.

Experienced and skilled journalists can command decent living wages. All branches of journalism are moderately peripatetic so the expert practitioner expects to establish a market value which is reasonably transportable to other magazines or companies. The true itinerant is not too popular in the trade since editors like a degree of stability in their staffing arrangements, but some movement of staff does occur and senior editorial salaries therefore tend to be market-driven.

Salaries in the mass-market consumer press are on average higher than among business and professional magazines although this is a dangerous generalisation because the high regard for 'flair' in this sector can lead to upwards distortion in a relatively small number of cases.

Very high salaries are unusual for magazine journalists, although editors of important magazines can command company director-level remuneration.

The 'meritocracy' system is equally a feature of other disciplines within a publishing company, including, for example, design and marketing.

In advertisement departments, the full fruits of one's labour are more quickly plucked since the employee's results are easily assessed and, because many companies base at least part of their sales people's packages on a turnover commission, some part of the ad salesman's income is under his own control.

In advertisement departments, therefore, higher salaries tend to come quicker but flatten out quicker too.

Senior managers – especially at board level – can earn substantial salaries and directors of large publishing companies can expect the usual competitive packages available to leaders throughout industry.

Those ambitious for great wealth will therefore need to determine to climb ever upwards through the organisation (or pursue a different career); those satisfied with a decent professional salary will achieve this on the basis of a tradesmanlike skill and some hard work.

'Representatives of the two teams must meet to reconcile their claims on the virgin leaves of the magazine.'

3
How a magazine is published: systems and jobs

THERE ARE FEW business activities where, when the end result of commercial enterprise is a saleable product, the product is essentially different every time it is produced.

The record industry is a good example. There are a few others. Magazine publishing is one of them.

When this is the case, the concept of 'making it happen' inevitably bears an implication of endeavour above and beyond the sedulous application of techniques learned, rules drawn up or systems invented. In some degree or another, particular individual creativity is an integral part of the process and must be accommodated within the commercial and manufacturing system . . . with all the difficulty and heartache that implies.

The evolution of magazine publishing practice has resulted in a methodology which will cope with the often mutually opposing demands of advertisers, editorial personnel, the typesetting, reproduction and printing processes, the tyrannies of time and distance, the arithmetic of a highly intricate production process and the pressures o f a competitive marketplace. The result, inevitably, is a compromise, but one which must not be apparent to reader or advertiser.

Many decisions in the management of publishing activities involve the compromise least unacceptable to most people.

To achieve this relatively happy state there is no alternative but to run a machine in which the parts mesh together without too much grinding and friction even though it is expected to run flat out most of the time.

As corny and boring as it sounds, teamwork is what counts in magazine publishing.

How the team is organised and which position each member plays varies considerably from magazine to magazine and from market sector to market sector. Women's magazines have staffing structures which are quite dissimilar from the arrangement of jobs on professional and business periodicals, and the skills and preoccupations of the staff are significantly different. But some factors are common to most magazines and it is worth trying to identify these and outline the types of activities, the routines and systems, which result in a product which is recognisable by the man in the street as a 'magazine'.

The profit motive

Firstly, most magazines are published for profit.

It is therefore helpful if the total costs of production including the overheads (the staff costs, accommodation, rent, light, heat, etc) as well as the manufacture are less than the combined revenues derived from advertising and the sale of copies.

Much of the effort which goes into producing a magazine is aimed at achieving this result and this is where apparently different disciplines within the publishing system are in fact inextricably linked.

A simplistic example is the final deadline for advertising copy: the date given to an advertiser as the final possible time for insertion of his advert into a specific issue. It is possible that a weekly magazine with very late deadlines for accepting classified jobs ads could gain an advantage over a competitor who cannot accommodate late advertisements. But this is an advantage which will cost something somewhere else in the publishing system. It could be that additional typesetting charges will be incurred, that editorial pages will be 'dropped' at the last minute to make room for the ads, that the magazine will appear on the bookstalls or reach the subscribers later than its competitor due to a later press run or that additional production and distribution costs will be involved in preventing this late delivery.

Several members of staff with different responsibilities within the publishing organisation will need to reach an accommodation, guided (hopefully) by someone senior in the management of the company. Involved in the arrangements will be the advertising staff who want to sell the 'late ads', advertisement production staff who need to get them typeset and made up into pages, editorial staff who must sacrifice deathless prose to make way for paying customers, a designer who is required to re-make the savaged editorial pages, circulation staff worried to death that the magazines won't reach the bookstalls on time and the production manager faced with the prospect of printing and binding his magazine significantly faster than usual in the face of a printer who is already running his machines in the red zone on the revolutions gauge.

It is the skill and professional quality of these people which will determine the success or failure of such an initiative.

The jobs

What are these people's jobs and how do they fit into the scheme of things?

It is helpful to have a hypothetical vehicle for all this trauma, and for this purpose I propose to resurrect a brave weekly venture first tortured into life in my book *Magazine and Journal*

Production for a similar purpose.

Despite the fierce competiton in the market for computer magazines, we have launched yet another title, the inventively-named *Computing Update*. As a weekly, it will face a few problems monthlies don't have but many of the characteristics of its publishing cycle will be common to monthlies.

Computing Update has an editorial staff of 12 (including a Picture Researcher), an Advertisement Manager and three salesmen, a Circulation Manager and three salesmen, a Promotions Manager, a Production Manager and a Production Controller, a Designer, an Accountant and two bookkeepers, They all answer to a Publisher.

(These staff numbers have been arbitrarily decided, regardless of the likely workload of this magazine, to create identifiable jobs rather than to achieve correct staffing levels and they assume no use of any available group publishing services.)

The magazine is A4 sized, typically about 128 pages in extent and sells 50,000 copies a week – 30,000 on bookstalls and 20,000 by subscription. It carries four-colour on some of the editorial pages and some of the advertising pages. It has a large section of classified advertisements for job vacancies.

The content of a magazine derives from two principal sources: the advertisement department and the editorial team.

There may be different types of advertisement and varying sorts of editorial matter and there may be sub-departments within those departments to cater for this but most of the printed material will be appearing at the instigation of the Editor or his nominee(s) or the Advertisement Manager or his nominee(s).

The system

Both teams will have been actively gathering material long before the week in which an issue appears.

'Early' editorial 'copy' will have been commissioned months in advance, will have been written by contributors, edited by editors, typeset, proof-read, corrected and made up into pages designed by a designer or by a specialist member of the editorial team. As the deadline for the issue approaches, later news copy will be written by freelancers or staff reporters, sub editors will edit this and fit it into pages, possibly working right up to the day the magazine goes to press.

Meanwhile, advertisement sales staff will have sold 'space' for that issue. Some of their sales will be 'series bookings' for an agreed number of insertions of advertisements in several issues; some will be one-off sales for one insertion; some will be bookings taken well in advance; some will be last-minute panics to get an ad into an issue at the eleventh hour. Classified advertisement sales staff will be making telephone calls, getting orders and copy by phone or chasing up regular advertisers who need reminding of ever-impending deadlines.

Somehow all this activity must be channeled into the structure of a printable magazine, so at the beginning of the production cycle of an issue, representatives of the two teams must meet to reconcile their claims on the virgin leaves of 'the book'. Short of a violent altercation, how is this achieved for *Computing Update*?

Like most delicate negotiations, it happens in stages.

A common starting point is an agreed ratio of editorial to advertising pages. In any magazine which relies significantly on advertising revenue in its profit mix, there must be some agreed relationship between the number of editorial pages which can be 'supported' by advertising revenue. This frequently takes the form of a ratio or percentage of advertising pages to editorial pages. The opening shot is therefore normally fired by the advertisement department in the form of a list, which reveals the number and shape of spaces so far booked for that issue, the restrictions on where these ads can or cannot be placed and their special requirements in terms of colour.

Due to the vagaries of the print production process, some

technical knowledge will now be needed to determine how the ads and editorial pages can be ordered into a sequence which is logical, aesthetic and still capable of being printed for less than the cost of a king's ransom and on *Computing Update* the production department will be responsible for proposing a solution in the form of a 'flat plan': a diagrammatic representation of the printing sequence of the pages of the magazine.

To prepare this, the production staff need to understand how the pages will be positioned on the printing machine and how the sections from this machine will be folded ready for binding – the 'imposition'.

One of the details provided by this knowledge will be the 'printable pagination' of the magazine: the different paginations it is technically possible or economic to print, given the multiples of pages produced by a printing press. To achieve an economic multiple of pages for the size of the magazine, some compromise will be necessary on how many pages of editorial and advertising can be carried, and this decision is left until the last possible moment.

Computing Update, which is published on Fridays, accepts its final display advertisement booking Tuesday 10 days before publication, its final display copy (the actual material to be printed) Friday, a week before publication, and its final classified advertisement copy Monday 5pm before publication.

Today is Tuesday, 10 days before publication, so theoretically we have all the display advertisement orders to hand. The Editor already has an agreed minimum allocation of editorial pages and has been told where his maximum dozen pages of colour can be positioned in the magazine. Now the production department can have a stab at telling the Editor how many pages in total are needed from him to fill the magazine to the agreed ratio of advertising:editorial. To make it easy for ourselves, we'll agree that the magazine works to a 50:50 ratio.

The list of display advertisements adds up to 32 pages in

all. Additionally the production controller knows that the classified advertisement section, although it can vary by up to 10 pages a week, is currently running at about 30 pages a week and this is the best guess the advertisement department can offer him so far ahead of the final classified advertising deadlines.

Being reasonably numerate, he tots up the figures and deduces that he has 62 pages of advertising. Another small sum tells him that to achieve a 50:50 ratio he must print 62 pages of editorial. For technical reasons, he knows it will be uneconomic to print 124 pages so he decides to ask the Editor for a further four editorial pages (totalling an issue size of 128 pages), having reached an accommodation with the Editor that, if the classified advertisements overrun by up to four pages, the Editor will carry four of his pages over to next week's issue.

Flexibility

In practice, unless the planning of the magazine is highly contentious, this first attempt at pagination can be made from lists supplied by the advertisement and editorial personnel with a minimum of debate . . . but I have referred to this as a first stage, and the reason for this pessimism is because there are very few magazines where these initial assumptions do not change as the production cycle continues.

Display advertisements may be cancelled or change size. Colour requirements may change. Extra bookings may come in. The root cause for this uncertainty is that most modern magazines, whether they are monthlies or weeklies, find it commercially advantageous to 'stay open' for advertisement orders beyond the date when it is first necessary to start planning the issue.

This is particularly true of classified advertisements, where on some magazines the pagination allocated at the time of the initial flat plan may bear only a passing resemblance to the final make-up of this section. On a weekly magazine like *Computing Update*, which obtains much of its revenue from this source, the classified ad section is indeed often considered quite separately and planned separately as a self-contained section of the magazine.

Editorial needs may also change, either of their own initiative or because, in re-arranging content to accommodate advertising, there is a knock-on effect elsewhere in the book.

Throughout the production cycle there will be a more or less constant requirement to make unplanned changes. This is in the nature of the business.

There will be changes to the pagination of the magazine, changes to the editorial content, changes in the number and type of adverts, minor (we hope) changes to schedules, changes of design, and so on. True, such aberrations are theoretically avoidable. But without them, on publication day, we would have a less interesting and useful magazine and probably a less profitable one.

In the case of our computer magazine, we will find:

1. That the pictures of the Ministry of Defence's showpiece computer installation, promised to the Picture Researcher by an optimistic press officer, have been withdrawn for 'security reasons' by his masters. A double-page spread has become a 500 word unillustrated article.

2. That the front cover design (already running a little behind schedule due to a recalcitract illustrator delivering his artwork late) is rejected by the Editor. Colour artwork which by 5.00pm Tuesday should have been undergoing the mysterious processes necessary for colour reproduction, will now have to be re-worked by the disgruntled designer who will burn the midnight oil to produce it by first thing Wednesday.

3. That a VDU manufacturer who had booked a series of half-page display ads, has withdrawn his bookings due

to an unfortunate slip-up the previous week when his logo was printed in the wrong shade of red.

4. That IBM have suddenly announced the launch of a new model of their PC. The News Editor wants to get a picture and story into this week's issue by re-jigging page 15.

5. That IBM want to replace their full-page ad (which normally carries the same message every week) with artwork announcing their new PC. This is at the moment in the hands of the printer of another computer magazine and arrangements must be made to get it into the *Computing Update* system.

6. That there is industrial action scheduled for British Rail Southern Region starting Wednesday midnight. If the deliveries can be re-scheduled to get the 'Southern' copies away first instead of last, distribution chaos can be averted.

. . . and so on.

Continuing activity

Meanwhile, sales of advertising and generation of early editorial material for future issues continue apace.

Meanwhile, also, the Circulation Manager and his staff are in constant liaison with wholesalers and bookstores, keeping track of orders and returns (unsold copies sent back), totting up the printing numbers for the week's issue, arranging the production of labels for the magazine bundles, deciding the order in which they will be sent out by rail or road, entering new subscriptions onto the computer system, printing out subscription labels for the postal copies, and so on.

And in the Promotions Department, computer listings are being analysed to identify prime targets for mailshots, an exhibition stand is being organised so that the magazine can present its face to the public at a forthcoming computer show, an itinerary is being arranged for the Editor to talk at a computing conference, a deal is being done with a computer books publisher to sell copies of these books through the magazine at a discounted price.

In the Production Department, invoices are being authorised, future flat plans are being prepared, tardy suppliers are being castigated, paper supplies are being ordered.

And in the Accounts Department, we hope that the sum total of entries in the sales ledger exceeds those in the purchase ledger.

To return to our original theme: because every edition of the magazine is different, all these jobs are interdependent. The content changes all the time and no systems run themselves as they might in a well-ordered manufacturing environment. Each job supports the others.

We look at these jobs in more detail in the following pages.

A high degree of literacy is desirable.

4
Editorial

IT IS TEMPTING to want all editorial staff to be possessed of remarkable literary powers but in practice the publisher wants a balance comprising a decent facility with words and some other important but fairly basic qualities.

The famous newspaper editor, Arthur Christiansen, when asked what he sought in a good reporter, said 'commonsense and commitment'. One of the training experts interviewed for this book commented: 'I'm not in search of great creative writing, although I do want a good level of literacy.'

No doubt Christiansen would have added a few extras to the cv of his ideal reporter if he didn't have other things on his mind at the time and no doubt the training expert would really be delighted to discover a remarkable creative potential if he stumbled across it alongside some more mundane qualities, but both were at pains to emphasise the balanced nature of the talent necessary to fill the pages of the press.

This is good or bad news to the editorial aspirant, depending on his particular proclivities, but it is important at the outset to realise that printing presses, like time itself, wait for no man (at least, not for long) and the job of the editorial staffer on a magazine is first and foremost to be reliable.

Reliability in this context implies the acquisition of skills developed to a degree where they are almost second nature and are readily at the disposal of the journalist, and − to use

Christiansen's word – the commitment to see a project through against the obstacles presented by passing time and the limitations of other men and their machines.

In considering what these disciplines comprise, generalisations are unavoidable and should be interpreted intelligently if applied to the editorial arrangements on specific magazines: job titles vary from periodical to periodical and so does the allocation between jobs of editorial responsibilities, but many principles are general throughout the industry and it is these we will try to identify.

It is, of course, a good idea if a member of an editorial team has writing talent and certainly he should be highly literate. The vital skill is the ability to write clear, concise, grammatical English which does not come between the reader and his understanding of the subject and preferably enhances his prospect of grasping the detail of a story or feature. Much of the training of journalists as writers, therefore, is dedicated to the logical arrangement of ideas and facts and the avoidance of convoluted forms of expression.

To achieve this facility presupposes the competence of the journalist himself to understand the subject and the needs of the market he is addressing.

Keeping in balance these two requirements – acquired knowledge and the skill to pass this on – is one of the most difficult tasks for those who employ magazine journalists and it is the reason why much recruitment of magazine editorial staff can occasionally appear somewhat eccentric.

Selecting staff

In this respect magazines are necessarily more adventurous than newspapers in their methods of selecting editorial staff.

Newspapers deal for the most part in general news and require most of their writers and editors to possess the skills necessary to report and comment on current affairs. There is a fairly well-refined system of training for newspapermen which concentrates on developing the knowledge needed to understand the workings of the main sources of current affairs news: government, courts, public services, and so on.

Most magazines, by comparison, are specialist publications which need at least some of their staff to have or acquire a detailed knowledge of their subject-matter.

It is desirable that a reporter on our magazine dealing with computing, for example, knows an Apple Mac from an IBM PC. This knowledge may be shared by a general news reporter on a daily paper, but the specialist should also be intimately acquainted with the full range of IBM PCs and the various models and options available from Macintosh so that he can immediately judge the significance of the release of a new machine and report on it in detail and in context. This would be a difficult task for the general news reporter unless he were technically competent to undertake considerable research.

The publisher of *Computing Update* seeking a reporter has two courses open to him:

1. To employ a general news reporter and train him in the mysteries of computer science.
2. To employ a computer expert and train him to be a journalist.

He may do either.

The principle is equally true of other editorial jobs. The requirement for specialist knowledge is most urgent in the case of the writer – who represents, as it were, the front line in the interpretation of information, but the editing and presentation of the text also require a sympathy with and knowledge of the content.

Let's look at the range of editorial jobs and what is involved in the processing of this knowledge into readable pages.

Reporters and writers

Daily newspapers, radio and television are in some degree in competition in the purveying of news since all three media are, theoretically at least, in the business of offering their audience the first intimation of the occurrence of an event.

Magazines are in a slightly different position since the frequency of publication is not adequate to carry 'hot' news in quite the same way.

If news is that which is 'new' to the reader of a magazine, it is likely to fall into one of three categories:

1. It is an event of universal interest but its occurrence is for some reason known only to the magazine.

2. It is an account of an event already noted but which includes additional detail of interest to a specialised readership.

3. It is the first intimation of an event which is so specialised that the general media have not mentioned it.

Successfully publishing news in all three categories requires (a) an intimate knowledge of the magazine's market and what will interest it, (b) the contacts, routines and instincts which will get the news and (c) the technical skills to write it and present it.

The good journalist is therefore someone who knows his readership, understands how to get his hands on information which is of interest to those readers and is capable of writing and/or editing this into a form which grabs attention and is easily digestible.

The first quality may be inherent if the journalist is already a specialist in the area of the magazine's market; if not, he must become immersed in the interests and concerns of his readership and must absorb all he can of the ethos of his publication. This is quite a challenge for even the most experienced of reporters.

The second ability – to get hold of the news – is in large degree a question of professionalism.

News comes into a magazine in many different ways: as a result of routine covering of events; in press releases; as a tip-off from a contact; as a follow-up of an earlier happening; as an investigation of something unusual or inconsistent; as the result of an inquiry about why something hasn't happened, and so on. Magazine editorial offices have systems and routines to process most of these sources and the principles of covering them can be taught.

The professional practices range from keeping a 'diary' of forthcoming events and making fine judgements about which are worth covering and in what detail through the business of making regular calls to worthwhile contacts to probing deeper than may be thought necessary into an apparently routine event.

As ever, particular qualities of individuals are important. The reporter with the curiosity and the stamina to pursue a lead even when the research becomes tedious or protagonists in the story become obstructive will be the leader of the pack at this stage and if, additionally, his judgment is sound, will bring back the bacon significantly more often than his colleagues, and his magazine will steal a march on its competitors.

Processing the information gathered requires a set of skills which involve damned hard work at the outset but which, when properly learned, become semi-automatic.

The reporter must be taught how to record information: shorthand is an invaluable tool, tape recorders are often used, and sensibilities need to be developed to understand the circumstances in which different techniques are appropriate.

Writing skills appropriate to the periodical must be developed. House style must be learned (the unique set of spelling, grammatical and punctuation rules peculiar to the publication). The business of re-writing press releases and handouts must be mastered. Telephone skills must be acquired. Interviewing techniques must be worked out. Press conference methods and systems must be understood. And so on.

Many of these aspects of the journalist's job draw particularly on personal qualities. Interviewing technique, for example, is partly governed by the reporter's own personality: whether he can make the subject feel relaxed and reassured that he will be properly represented. Confidence is an important attribute and the shy trainee has a particularly difficult hurdle to jump.

In terms of the working day of the reporter, the sorts of activities mentioned above may be represented in any sort of mixture depending on the type of magazine he is working on, the number of reporters employed, their respective responsibilities and his own particular talents. Much or little time may be spent out of the office; varying periods may be spent researching, interviewing and writing.

The journalist who has a particular facility with words and the ability to study subjects 'in depth' may find he is best suited to feature writing: the preparation of longer articles which analyse the background to the news or present a detailed consideration of a subject. It is not unusual for such work to become the province of one or more editorial staffers.

Similarly, those with highly specialised knowledge of the magazine's subject areas may find themselves employed as 'specialist' or 'technical' writers, responsible for covering complex matters in some detail.

Usually, such roles evolve as the journalist demonstrates the balance of his abilities.

Where there are several reporters working together there may be a Chief Reporter and/or News Editor responsible for allocating work to the team, deciding on priorities and the significance of stories, administrating the newsgathering routines, and so on.

Sub editors

Sub editors also often (but not necessarily) start life as reporters.

The responsibilities of a 'sub' vary considerably from magazine to magazine but at their most basic usually encompass most of the following:

- Editing copy for readability and grammatical propriety.
- Correcting spelling mistakes.
- Ensuring conformity to house style.
- Marking up copy with typographical commands for the typesetter.
- Working out the length of a piece of text and if necessary cutting it to fit.
- Writing headlines to fit in specified sizes of type.
- Writing cross heads, sub heads, side heads, captions for pictures, etc.
- Proof reading and correction.

And maybe:

- Assessing the relative merits of different pieces and deciding their position in the magazine.
- Designing pages or ensuring typographical conformity to a design.
- Selecting and rejecting illustrations, sizing them up and marking them properly for the printer to originate.

The sub editor therefore needs both an editorial facility and a good knowledge of typography and printing processes. In writing a headline, for example, he must be able to come up with a strong, attention-commanding line which properly represents the content of the story it heads but he must do this within the space available according to the size of type dictated by the design of the page.

Because he is also in some measure in control of other people's work and has the authority to edit it, he must also have some sensibility. As one American editor expresses the point: 'Sensibility is absolutely essential. Without it, the editor with a script is like an ape with an oboe: you can be sure no good will come of it, and the most you can hope for is to get it back intact.'

However, the sub is also ideally creative. His function should include the possibility of working up a story to make the most of all its potential, identifying missed or under-developed angles and generally using an objective eye and professional skill to enhance the readability of the text.

The range of activities pursued by the sub will depend on the structure within the editorial office. In many cases there will be a 'chief sub editor' or a 'production editor' (or maybe both) who carry some of the burden and possibly other editors with specialist responsibilities.

Editors and The Editor

The Chief Sub may be responsible for allocating work to a team of sub editors, producing the editorial part of the 'flat plan' mentioned in chapter three (i.e. deciding, probably in consultation with the Editor, what goes where), and generally acting as the arbiter of professional taste when it comes to copy editing decisions.

The Production Editor may be responsible for some of these matters and/or the maintenance of the schedules which determine which parts of the magazine 'go to bed' (are made up into pages and 'passed for press') at which stage in the production cycle. He will liaise with other departments in the magazine – advertising, production, design – to co-ordinate activities.

There may be other editors or editorial staff with specialised jobs – for example, a Features Editor and a Picture

Researcher – who have clearly defined responsibilities and who must communicate closely with their colleagues to ensure the editorial content comes together in as orderly a fashion as possible.

On *Computing Update*, there may additionally be, for instance, a Software Editor with the responsibility for monitoring the release of new software, reporting on important issues, compiling lists of new programs coming onto the market, commissioning reports on significant developments and acting as the expert advisor in this field to the other editorial staff.

These specialist roles may embrace quite different levels of responsibility and authority on different magazines and the division of labour into these jobs may be extreme or virtually non-existent.

The structure in the editorial office may in fact range from a one-man band reporting, subbing and editing to put together a small quarterly at the modest end of the scale to a large staff of reporters, editors and specialists on a big monthly consumer magazine or a weekly news mag.

But whatever the size of the outfit, almost inevitably at the head of the team, large or small, is someone with ultimate power and responsibility as far as the editorial staff are concerned: the Editor.

The Editor

Editors producing magazines are rather like ships' captains on voyages. Their powers don't quite extend to conducting marriage ceremonies for members of the crew, but in many other respects they have the same extensive and somewhat autocratic potential to build and develop a team and govern the activities of the players.

The naval captain may have some concern about what the pen-pushers back in the Admiralty will think when they hear how he has conducted matters on his latest expedition and the Editor may need to pursuade the management of a publishing company that the most recent edition of his magazine is well-founded. But in each case there is only a limited influence which can be brought to bear once the vessel is under sail.

The ship is too far from home and the magazine is too far advanced in its production cycle at any one stage for anyone other than the skipper or the editor respectively to make fundamental decisions about the course to be steered.

In practice, the Editor is interpreting the strategic plans of his directors or proprietors just as the Captain is pursuing a government's military policies.

The first requirement of an Editor, therefore, is that he understands the business and publishing strategy of his company and is in sympathy with it, i.e. that he thinks it is a proper role for the magazine and that it will work in terms of building up circulation and attracting advertising.

In this context, the Editor is in a broad sense also a contributor to the management of the company and it is normally expected that his views will be influential in deciding policy.

His other tasks are very wide-ranging.

He is, as we have noted, the manager of his staff. On some magazines he may have departmental heads in the shape of the Production Editor, Features Editor and so on reporting to him while on others he may be the only head of department for all the editorial staff. He should also be an expert on his readership: who his readers are and the matters which concern them. He should interpret to his staff (and seek their views on) his vision of the role of the magazine. He is the staff's top-level link with the rest of the management of the company. He will probably also be something of an expert on the systems of producing his magazine. And on a small magazine he may perform some or all of the roles of other members of staff outlined earlier in this chapter.

The balance of an Editor's responsibilities is largely

determined by the size and type of the magazine he edits. On a small magazine, as we have noted, he may be tied to his desk shuffling paper, editing copy, liaising with contacts, and so on: in practice, a combination of reporter, sub editor and editor.

On a large and influential magazine he may delegate practically all the day-to-day production of the issue to others and may devote much of his time to making high-level contacts in the magazine's areas of influence, developing strategic plans for its greater glory and possibly involving himself deeply in its financial progress. Such editors are sometimes directors of the companies which employ them, although it is not unusual for both editors and boards of directors in these circumstances to feel that editors should not be directors: that it circumscribes their editorial prerogative sometimes to pursue policies which are not immediately beneficial in business terms.

These are sophisticated considerations; what we should observe here is that the role of a magazine editor can be essentially functional in the production of the periodical or it can be more in the style of a figurehead representing the purpose and influence of the publication.

In either circumstance, the editor must be a strong personality who is confident of his aspirations for the magazine and his ability to achieve them.

Not all good reporters or sub editors make good editors because the personal qualities necessary to lead a team and implement a publishing plan are not necessarily those required to report on events, process copy or work out the technical details of an issue going to press. Similarly, as we shall see in a later chapter, not all good editors make good leaders of publishing companies.

What is true, however, is that the editor who has a command of some of the technical skills needed to process a magazine through to publication is more likely to win the confidence of his staff and to achieve his own goals without needing to learn the mysteries of publishing systems and practices.

Many editors consequently have come up through the reporting-sub editing route and are skilled journalists in their own right.

A dying breed: the foot-in-the-door salesman of yesteryear is being replaced by highly trained staff with the intellect to present a plausible marketing case.

5
The Advertisement Department

ADVERTISING has become a very sophisticated business.

The range of media has widened dramatically in recent years, so has the size of the cake to be divided and so have the techniques used.

We have seen in the opening chapter that the magazine press is doing a good job holding its own in this highly competitive environment. This has been achieved by keeping pace with change and adopting an intelligent and resourceful approach to the evolving scene. The corollary of this proposition is that the people involved in the game need to be of a higher calibre than ever before.

'Selling space', as the trade jargon has it, is no longer the job of the foot-in-the-door fast talker. A high degree of professionalism is the order of the day.

We will examine this challenge and the tasks involved in meeting it, but first let's take a quick look at the structure of the business as far as magazines are concerned.

Clients, agencies and the media

We can all readily understand who *clients* are: they are the real advertisers – people with something to sell. This may be virtually anything from a bicycle to a new model from Rolls Royce, from a job vacancy to a new image for a large company. The client may be a housewife placing a one-off classified ad or a multi-national corporation booking a whole series of display advertisements as part of a fabulously expensive marketing campaign.

We are all likely to be advertisers at least once in our lives and we are all likely to work for organisations which advertise their products or services.

We can also all readily identify the *media*: as far as we are concerned at present, the media is periodicals – regularly appearing publications which carry the advertisements the clients wish to place.

So what are the *agencies*, and what do they do?

Well, in the first place, they are not all what they once were. A little history is helpful.

Some agencies originally sold space on behalf of magazines. They worked on a commission basis, were financial 'middle men' (responsible to the magazine for handling the invoicing, collecting the money and were legally at risk for the advertisers' debts), and liaised between the advertiser and the magazine.

Gradually these services increased to embrace a full-scale representation of the advertiser's interest, planning his campaign, preparing and producing the advertisements, buying all his space from the media, and so on. In a real sense, the advertiser became the client's agent.

Today, this type of agency is known as a 'full service agency', although there are other types offering more restricted services (for example, 'media independents' providing only the media buying part of the operation). Full service agencies generally charge a commission of 15%, which comes off the price of the advertisement. The magazine selling to or receiving copy from a full service agency expects all the creative work to have been handled in advance. The agency represents the client and should provide advertisements in the form the magazine requires for production.

There are many variations on the role of the agency and the services it offers, which we have no space to explore here; it is enough to bear in mind that in many instances the space salesman on a magazine will be dealing with a large, professional organisation which has extensive market research and creative resources and which will expect an equally professional approach from the salesman.

Classified ads

There are two broad categories of advertising pages carried in magazines: *classified* and *display*.

Classified ads are those which are physically grouped together in the book and organised into classifications: situations vacant, cars for sale, houses for sale, services, personal, and so on. Within the classified pages themselves there are often three types of 'space': *lineage, semi-display* and *display*. Lineage are those ads which run on in closely set lines in single columns and are charged according to the number of words contained in the advertisement. Semi-display may occupy more than one column and are charged at a rate per single column centimetre. Display ads will typically be boxed-in with borders or rules and contain artwork of some kind (often the logo of the company advertising); they are charged by the single column centimetre or by set sizes made available for this type of ad.

The rate card for a classified section in *Computing Update* will look something like this:

Classified Advertisement Pages
Display
£20 per single column centimetre
Quarter page: £500
Half page: £900
Full page: £1,800

Semi-display
£17 per single column centimetre

Lineage
50p per word
Box number: £3.00 extra

Often the typesetting and make-up of such ads is handled by the magazine itself (or its production suppliers) and is included in the cost of the advertisement.

Some magazines, especially in the consumer group areas, carry no classified ads to speak of, but in the professional and business press, where a trade magazine may be an important vehicle for announcing new job vacancies, classified advertising can be a highly profitable element in a magazine's financial make-up and a major ingredient in its *raison d'etre* for both the proprietors and the readers. The pages of situations vacant in a trade magazine may well be as earnestly thumbed-through by the readers as the editorial pages, and their *content* as well as their *revenue* can be vital to the appeal of the magazine.

In some instances, the magazine with the most situations vacant in its classified ad section may end up as the de facto market leader.

This theme of the reader-pulling power of advertising is noteworthy and is touched-on again later. The instance of job vacancies is a readily-understandable example of the phenomenon.

Display ads

Display ads are those which appear in individual positions throughout a magazine and can only be booked in set sizes. For example, a magazine may make space available to advertisers in the following increments:

Full page
Half page vertical
Half page horizontal
Quarter page
Eighth page

Unlike classified ads, much of the display material may be accommodated within the editorial sections of the magazine (although a few publications keep it separate) and it is often possible to reserve special positions (e.g. 'facing editorial matter', 'facing contents page', 'back cover', 'right-hand page facing editorial', and so on).

Some bookings may also be for 'series' of ads throughout a year or part of a year and therefore forming a fundamental plank in an advertiser's future marketing strategy. Bookings like this will attract a 'series discount'.

The rate card for display ads in *Computing Update* will look something like this:

Display Advertisements

Page: £900
Half page: £500
Quarter page: £300
Eighth page: £200

Guaranteed positions
Page: £1,000
Half page: £600

Covers
(Complete page, 4-colour only)
Inside front: £1,500
Outside back: £1,600

Colour
Spot colour: £250 extra
Full colour: £500 extra

Series discount
7 insertions: 5%
13 insertions: 10%
26 insertions: 15%

Spot colour, as mentioned above, is the term for a single colour printed on specified areas of text, and used to attract attention or enhance the appearance of an advertisement.

As noted in Chapter 3, a complicated juggling act with the arrangement of each issue of the magazine is caused by requirements for special positions, colour, and so on.

Most display ads in magazines come through agencies and the material for these arrives in a suitable form for printing using the particular technical resources available to the publications in which they are to appear. In a few instances, usually in specialist publications, a small advertiser may wish to deal direct and the magazine may help him prepare his material, and in a few cases where very high quality magazines are being produced to very demanding technical standards, the publishers may insist that part of the technical preparation of the material is handled by the magazine itself to ensure consistency of reproduction.

Both these circumstances are, however, unusual.

The agency obtains its knowledge about how to prepare its material for a specific magazine from two principal sources: the magazine's 'rate card' (which lists its prices for space and the technical specification of the production requirement) and from a regular publication called *British Rate and Data* (*BRAD*), which contains roughly the same information for every major magazine in the UK.

This takes the form of some technical mumbo-jumbo which,

in the case of *Computing Update*, might look something like this:

Mechanical data: Type page size 266x178. Half 266x87 or 133x178. Quarter 133x87. Trim size 297x210. Bleed page 310x220. Allow 6mm down backs for perfect binding. Screened positive litho film, right-reading emulsion side down, same size with proof or complete artwork for web offset printing. Screen 40, cover and full colour 54. Number of classified columns: 4. Classified column length: 266. Width: 43. 2 cols: 87.5. 3 cols: 132.5. 4 cols: 178. Film to FIPP specifications. Insert specification on application.

Selling space

Advertisers are not fools; nor are agencies. Contrary to popular belief, advertisements are not placed in magazines because a fast-talking rep bought a big lunch for someone or because a media buyer had an instinctive feeling that this would be a 'good place' to advertise.

The analysis of the results obtained from advertising in different media and from advertising in different places within one branch of the media is now very sophisticated. The results are measured very carefully and decisions are made with a considerable degree of cool, scientific calculation about likely future benefit. Market research and statistical analysis play an increasingly large part in the agency world and magazines which cannot justify their existence in well-explained, logical terms which can satisfy the media buyer sitting on a stack of facts and figures about the competitors had better shut up shop soon.

A magazine's advertisement department has always had a demanding but fascinating challenge: to put together a case which bears close examination for why their magazine is the place to advertise a product or service and then to go out and sell that case for all it's worth.

In recent years, the first part of that task has become more important.

It has long been possible to reach some reasonably reliable conclusions about how many copies of a magazine go out into the marketplace and who is reading them. To determine a cost per *reader* reached is not difficult. Organisations like the Audit Bureau of Circulations (ABC), to which most magazines belong, verify sales statistics and print audited results. The Joint Industry Committee of the National Readership Survey (JICNARS) samples readership. Other organisations conduct clever surveys using a variety of statistical parameters.

But increasingly advertisers want to know the cost per *buyer* and much effort is going into producing the data which will give this figure.

Trends, also, are important because fashions and the media are ever changing.

The ad department's job is therefore becoming more scientific, more market research is being conducted by magazines themselves and more attention is being paid to preparing the correct information to persuade an agency that *this* is the right place to advertise a product or service on the basis of the data produced.

The industry is recruiting a different type of salesman.

The new sales people

More and more graduates are joining magazines as advertisement representatives.

The demand for young people with the intellectual ability to join in on the new, scientific approach to advertisement marketing is high and will remain high because their counterparts in the advertisers' and agencies' media buying offices require a properly-presented, intelligently made out case for buying space in one publication rather than another.

The preparation of this case needs someone with the general intelligence to understand how fairly complicated sets of data can be analysed and used and with a sufficiently good education to help package the material up in an accessible form either to use as printed marketing aids or to present verbally over the media buyer's desk.

It also needs someone who is capable of understanding the magazine and its editorial strategy. Liaison with editors is necessary if the strengths of the magazine are to be recognised and exploited. How is the magazine different from its competitors and how can these differences be used?

Of course, the job is still that of a sales person because, when all the desk work has been done, the rate cards put together, the mailshots written and designed, the graphs drawn and the statistics compiled, someone has to go out into the market and sell. It is still true that, when all things are equal, a good sales rep can win an edge over his competitors.

And selling requires some special personal qualities. It is in some ways a lonely job when closing the sale is up to one individual's persuasiveness. It is a job which needs self-motivation and it is a job which demands a resilient spirit because there will always be failures.

A strong, extrovert personality must support the professionalism and marketing skills.

Learning the trade

Some advertisement sales people come into magazines from local or national newspapers, where they have learned the elements of the job and then set about absorbing the differences between newspaper and magazine advertising.

Some enter the industry straight from school or university to sell display advertising, sit alongside other staff, go out with them to visit clients, attend courses and gradually achieve the professional skills to act independently.

Some answer advertisements in the national press for telephone salespeople and are trained to sell classified advertising by phone. They may then decide to move on to selling display space and learn the extra skills necessary to handle that new dimension.

All companies have their own methods of training in ad sales: usually a mixture of internal training, learning by experience alongside their experienced colleagues and attending special courses on sales technique and the technicalities of the magazine business in general.

Companies like Reed Business Publishing have highly structured internal courses which include carefully designed sessions of role playing – acting out situations and analysing performance in context – and other monitoring and situation-based approaches to sales techniques.

External courses include those organised by the Periodicals Training Council, referred to in chapter 11, and those run by the Communication, Advertising and Marketing Education Foundation (CAM), which is the examining board for vocational qualifications in these areas. CAM offers studies leading to a certificate-level qualification and diplomas at post-certificate-level in advertising, public relations and marketing.

Like all jobs in magazines, selling space is hard work but can result in great personal satisfaction. Success can be easily measured and the good representative is much admired. It is also a lively job, with display sales people spending a lot of their time out of the office, often forming close and enjoyable professional relationships with agencies and clients.

They also have the satisfaction of contributing to the copy sales of a magazine for they know that many readers are buying copies for the ads they contain as much as for the editorial content.

A cheerful personality and the ability to keep calm under pressure are useful qualities.

6
The Design Studio

TO BE CREATIVE under pressure is a testing challenge.

While it is true that much of the work that goes into planning the visual impact of a magazine relies on the routine exercise of a set of acquired skills, it is also the case that, throughout all branches of trade and industry, innovation in design and the intelligent application of design to enhance commercial potential has become critically important within an increasingly competitive business environment.

In the magazine industry, as elsewhere, standards of design have risen dramatically in response to this need.

Long-established magazines have been thoroughly revamped and many new magazines which are outstanding examples of imaginative graphic creativity have appeared.

Technology has also played a part in this revolution and has brought delights and dangers. New electronic methods of composing text and generating graphics have freed the designer from the chains of a mediaeval production system and have enabled a flexibility of interpretation without the former cost and time penalties which bedevilled the industry for so many years. But freedom, as always, imposes responsibilities – in this case, to use the wide range of techniques now available with proper discipline and with that elusive quality: good taste.

In some cases, it has also facilitated the direct use of graphic techniques without the intermediate and sometimes steadying intervention of tradesmen trained to strain publishers' requests through the sieve of industry traditions. Machines which were once the province of typesetters and other trade specialists can now sit on designers' desks, replacing the conventional tools of the trade and offering the immediate possibility of generating text and graphics to reproduction quality as part of the creative process.

We look more closely at this later in the chapter.

Meanwhile, we should note that graphic design is a skill in transition, both in terms of its significance and in its methods of practice.

The qualities needed

Magazines generally employ *graphic designers*, i.e. those who have been trained in typography and layout specifically for the production of printed materials. Art and printing colleges offer a range of courses in graphic design, leading to formal qualifications which are universally recognised.

At Reading College of Art and Technology, for example, there are two principal streams of training. School leavers with GCSEs can take a two-year Ordinary National Diploma course and can then go on to take a two-year Higher National Diploma Course; alternatively, there is a one-year foundation course followed by a BA degree.

Increasingly, magazines are employing designers with degree-level qualifications.

The first prerequistite, therefore, is formal training in graphic design to a good standard. Learning basic skills on the job is now unusual.

Secondly, there are specialised abilities which must form part of a general range of talents.

Good production knowledge is essential. Anyone working in a magazine studio must know the production implications arising from the processing of a graphic idea through the printing process. The cost of achieving an effect is important; so is the time it will take to process work in one way rather than another. Ideas can often be interpreted mechanically by a variety of methods and the popular worker will know how to select the method which holds down costs and facilitates, rather than hinders, production.

A good knowledge of typography is vital and a feeling for the use of typography – balance, weight and effect – is necessary. Much of this comes with experience, but the basic groundwork must have been done.

Similarly, a feeling for and knowledge of the use of colour are increasingly important in an industry which perceives the impact of colour as an integral ingredient in its presentation. Again, experience is necessary but a good colour sense must exist to be developed.

The creative and balanced use of images is also a challenge most magazine designers will face and enjoy if they are to be successful.

The potential recruit's portfolio will show examples of the good use of type in relation to images, preferably some colour work, an appreciation of production implications and some good routine skills, such as copyfitting (ensuring the text fits the space allocated to it). An ability to illustrate is not usually one of the talents demanded since most magazines put out illustration work to freelances.

It is also worth commenting that where an art department's brief includes work for conferences, exhibitions and promotions (see below) it may be helpful to have some experience of packaging and point of sale material.

Above and beyond this, a resilient personality is essential.

Demands on the designer's skill, energy and patience are constant. Everyone on a good magazine is in pursuit of excellence and this strains all professional relationships.

The soundest basis for handling this pressure is a commitment to producing a fine product within the parameters established by the commercial environment within which the staff are working. Common sense and a happy disposition will help to make the designer receptive to the pragmatic limitations of working with others who understand what they want but do not appreciate the technical possibilities and impossibilities.

On the positive side, the ability to sell ideas is helpful because many visual concepts need good salesmanship to those whose primary professional drives are usually interpreted textually. To be capable of discussing conceptual matters in an articulate fashion, to be able to describe visual ideas persuasively, is a facility well worth acquiring . . . and, incidentally, characteristic of many leading figures in the design world.

Who does what

As with many disciplines in magazine publishing, it is very difficult to give hard and fast guidelines about the sort of structure the newcomer is likely to find within any given company.

The conceptual design of a publication is often commissioned from an external source, maybe a high-profile magazine design group who will set aside the time and resources to re-examine the strategy of a periodical from an objective viewpoint and come up with a proposal for either a totally new look or an evolutionary modification which will bring the presentation into line with contemporary concepts. The day-do-day interpretation of that design might then be left to the staff of the magazine itself.

On certain types of magazine (mainly in the business press or specialised consumer titles) some or all of the pages are designed by editorial staff with special skills in page make-up. On others, all or some of the pages go through a design department.

The design department itself may be part of the editorial team or may be an entirely separate entity providing additional resources to other parts of the company, as with conference work, explained below.

Even when all pages go through the art studio, it may be the case that headlines are written or suggested by editorial, leaving it to the designers to complete the page designs, or matters can be arranged so that there is constant liaison between editorial and design, who work in close concert to achieve the desired result.

In the instance of *Computing Update*, the news pages, which are specified to a fairly standard format, are laid out by the News Editor, who has experience of this type of work, while the features pages are handled by the Design Studio who discuss the layout and headlines with the Features Editor. The Picture Researcher will also be in constant liaison with the Features Editor and the designers to ensure they have the visual material necessary to create lively and appropriate layouts.

Promotions, conferences, exhibitions

In chapter eight we will look at the marketing side of magazines and it will become clear that much time and energy goes into ensuring a high profile and generating additional sales.

All this may have a considerable impact on a design studio and may broaden its responsibilities into areas of point of sale design, packaging, advertisement design and exhibitions and conference display material.

Indeed, there may be a separate studio to handle this material.

The subjects involved may range from advertisement rate cards (often quite elaborate folders with inserted cards and enclosures) to the full-scale design and construction of an exhibition stand. The actual construction or decoration of exhibition stands may be required and – a constant theme – liaison with other parts of the company will be necessary to ensure the agreed themes to present the image of the magazine and its enterprises are pursued with a dynamic consistency.

In this, as in other areas of the studio's activity, commissioning work from outside sources will almost inevitably be part of the brief.

Commissioning work

There are few design studios which embrace all the talents necessary to provide a full service to all parts of a magazine company.

An example mentioned above is illustration. The drawing of illustrations, be they cartoons or finely detailed coloured artwork of considerable creative complexity, is often commissioned from outside sources because it is unusual that a magazine's facilities include either the skills or an appropriate environment for the production of this type of highly specialised work.

Even when suitable skills are available in-house, the uneven ebb and flow of work often dictates the necessity for outworking at least a part of the workload.

One of the important roles fulfilled by the studio is therefore the organised and imaginative commissioning of freelance work, scheduling and keeping track of its progress, and handling the paperwork which results from these activities.

Unless the unit is very small, this job is normally left to senior staff whose experience is considerable and whose judgement has been refined by years of patient toleration of the inability of all publishers to specify their requirements with any degree of precision. The challenge is to strike a balance between creativity and reliability: choosing contacts who will deliver the jobs they have promised with unfailing reliability while possessing the imagination to interpret often ill-expressed wishes with a fair chance of coming close to the aspirations of the editorial or marketing people.

This is, of course, a continuing theme of the designer's role but is particularly important when the facilities to modify and change an idea are physically remote.

Commissioning artwork is an art in itself; it is enough to note here that it is often a part of the studio's job and requires plenty of tact and experience.

New technology

Art colleges who are on the one hand pruning their slim budgets by cutting back on pens and board are at the same time struggling to find ways to raise the cash to install the microcomputers which are revolutionising the way graphic designers go about their business.

Within the remarkably short space of a few years, a new generation of graphics software, driven in the first place by some innovative technology by Apple Computers, has put within designers' reach the possibility of using computer-power to implement many of their visual concepts without recourse to the manual tools conventionally used.

'Paint' and 'draw' programs, combined with 'desktop publishing systems', enable the computer-literate designer to create a wide range of graphical effects on computer screen and print these out on laser printers or other devices. Much of this software is still in its evolutionary stage but has nevertheless passed through the experimental phase to become highly productive for straightforward work and the machines are fast being installed in publishers' offices.

There is little doubt that the designer who wishes to stay ahead of the field must make a friendly acquaintance with the hardware and software which, in future years, will be the main tools of the trade. This can be a potentially daunting prospect to the uninitiated but is in reality extremely exciting and absorbing, opening up many facilities to reduce the mundane aspects of generating type and graphics and providing almost limitless opportunities for experimentation and imaginative innovation.

As with many occupations, the manual skills required may be diminished but in return the possibilities for clearing time and space for truly creative work are greatly enhanced.

Something seems to go wrong with every issue.

7
The Production Department

AS WE HAVE SEEN in previous chapters, there is some variation, between different publishing companies, in the precise inter-departmental allocation of responsibilities. These varying routines are at their most disparate in the arrangements for control of production and the concept of what 'production' embraces, so it is necessary to consider explanations in the following text as a template which can be adapted to alternative structures rather than a universal system of control practised throughout the industry.

In the case of our archetypal magazine, *Computing Update*, I have assumed a separate production department with a structure fairly common in magazine publishing companies: a Production Manager who carries the can and one or more production controllers – trained specialists who understand the various technical processes involved in getting out a magazine.

There is a wide range of terminology alternatives. In large companies there is often a Production Director at board level and job titles such as Production Assistant, Production Executive, and so on. In some instances, there is no production department and the function is accommodated elsewhere in the structure. But this is now unusual.

Defining the role of the production department (if it exists) is partly a question of striking a balance between exercising a proper degree of control and allowing editorial and advertising procedures to go on unhindered by unnecessary bureaucracy. How to achieve this is a reasonable subject for debate within the structure of a particular magazine but some responsibilities are more or less standard and we'll take a look at those.

Print buying

Print buying includes the selection of suppliers of typesetting, the various processes which are necessary to convert text and pictures into a printable form (known as 'origination'), printing – of course – and paper. In this context the Production Manager needs both purchasing and technical skills, like many buyers in industry.

His job here is to understand the technical resources which are necessary to manufacture his magazine and to know which suppliers possess them. He must then negotiate a keen price for services which meet the demands of the editorial, advertising and circulation departments.

The manager himself is usually responsible for print buying decisions since many thousands of pounds' worth of purchasing commitment is at stake and to handle this well requires considerable experience of market prices, negotiating techniques, customary credit arrangements, and so on.

Estimating and costing

Since a magazine is a 'live' product which changes from issue to issue, there is a more or less constant demand for costing information as variations on the 'standard' issue occur or new projects are proposed. There is also a need to monitor costs closely and systematically.

The production department will work from sets of price scales provided by suppliers. These will itemise in some detail the costs attached to the many technical processes involved in the production of a publication.

A regular routine will be checking the suppliers' invoices which follow close on the heels of the publication of an issue and reconciling these with the actuality of the tasks performed on that issue. There will be queries to be settled, inconsistencies to be investigated and lessons to be learned from the appearance of costs which are higher than usual or unanticipated.

Since costs are simply a reflection of publishing decisions and the activities of staff in putting the magazine together, there will also be comments worth passing back to the departmental heads if uncomfortably high items appear on invoices.

Budgeting and forecasting

He who understands the costs can forecast the future, given the necessary assumptions from other departments. Magazine publishing, like all other businesses, requires plans to be made for years to come and part of this planning involves the preparation of information which reflects the costs associated with the management's ambitions.

So many pages of editorial will cost so much to typeset and print; so many advertisements will cost so much to carry; so many extra copies printed will add so much to the print bill; so much additional colour will bump up costs by so much. The usual routine for preparing budgets is for the management to agree a plan in the form of a series of assumptions about such items and for the production department to cost this out.

Future forecasts may cover the next year or the next few years. A 'five year plan' is not unusual (although it is unusual for its detail to come true in the fullness of time!).

Technical advice

Production staff are expected to be exponents of the art of the possible. Other departments need to know what can be done and how best it can be done, whether the points at issue are schedule changes or fancy reproduction. They look to the production department for information.

This clearly involves understanding not just the principles of the technical processes but also the facilities available at the magazine's suppliers and whether these can be supplemented from other sources if necessary. The publisher who is perverse enough to want a tube of lipstick fixed to the front cover of every women's magazine he issues will not be impressed if the production department tells him this is not possible because the printer hasn't got the resources. He will want to know how else it can be done, how long it will take and what the cost will be.

Everything is possible . . . at a price and in due course. The production department must discover the cheapest, quickest methods.

More mundane examples occur frequently. In many cases the production controller will know the answers by heart; in others he will need to do some research.

Scheduling

Experience is a great aid to devising a practical schedule and experience plus technical knowledge of what the men and machines can achieve tends to reside in the production department. There is often also a finer sense of balance here, editorial and advertising people leaning towards the optimistic in their assessment of the art of the possible.

Close consultation with other departments and maybe the involvement of some of the suppliers is necessary.

The object of the exercise is to get down on paper the

timing of the sequence of events which lead up to the publishing of the magazine. This can be a very complicated performance, given that several issues will be in production at any one time and various 'sections' of the magazine will be at different stages in the production cycle.

It is in the nature of the challenge that some re-adjustment is necessary from time to time as there are changes in the magazine itself or in its suppliers. The business of drawing up and monitoring schedules therefore continues more or less indefinitely on a lively magazine.

The flat plan

We saw in chapter three how a diagrammatic plan is produced for each issue of a magazine.

The flat plan may originate in the editorial or advertising departments or in the production department itself but certainly technical knowledge will be necessary to work out the positions in which certain pages can be printed within the overall scheme of the magazine. The way colour can be positioned within a magazine is dependent on the press being used and various other factors. This is one circumstance in which a technician's expertise is required to help make up the plan for 'the book'.

The least the production department is required to do is advise on possibilities and limitations; more usually, they are intimately involved in drawing up the flat plan.

Here again it should be emphasised that the ability to communicate effectively with other staff is absolutely as important as a detailed knowledge of the mechanical techniques involved. Whenever technology imposes limitations, there will be competing demands on the facilities available; the production controller will often find himself in the role of a first level arbitrator attempting to draw up a compromise solution to the problem of reconciling one department's requirements with another's in a situation in which the printing process can give neither exactly what it wants.

In such circumstances, which occur frequently in the production of a magazine, expertise and good judgment go hand in hand. The experienced and knowledgeable production man who has demonstrated that he is a master of his subject will gain the respect of those who are equally professional in other departments and the whole process of liaison will become easier as mutual trust is established.

Troubleshooting

When schedules break down or when disastrous misdemeanours are perpetrated by typesetter or printer it is not unreasonable that he who chose the suppliers helps to sort out the mess.

Because the production of a magazine is a volatile business, things go wrong with every issue. Some are more serious than others. Some are the fault of the publishing staff; some are the fault of suppliers; some are the result of sloppy systems; some are acts of God or some less benign power (the courier's motor cycle blows up on the way to deliver the final artwork to the printer).

Whatever the cause, the trouble must be investigated, rectified if possible, and hopefully prevented from recurring.

In an earlier chapter it was claimed that advertising salesmen must have some degree of personal resilience to the slings and arrows of outrageous fortune. The same is true of production staff. A weekly magazine may involve several hundred individuals in taking action which, if neglected or misdirected, can hold up production. It is human nature that every week someone somewhere will fail. The production controller will often be in the position of getting the show back on the road again.

Quality control

Some of the big magazine groups have – or had – quality control departments, but this is now changing, and production staff are usually considered the arbiters of quality disputes as well as the potential correctors. There is a certain illogicality in this – somewhat akin to a lawyer representing the prosecution and the defence – but given the need for technical know-how to dispute technical problems it is probably inevitable.

As mentioned above, the fulfilment of such a role becomes easier as a reputation for expertise and soundness of judgment is established. The true wisdom of the production expert in this function is to establish why things went wrong and prevent their recurrence. Often quality problems can be resolved in future; often they are simply human error. Energy is needed to deal with the former; discretion and maybe tough-mindedness is required in the latter case.

Arranging logistics

In this context 'logistics' is used to describe the devising and controlling of the various physical systems for the transfer of materials and information from place to place necessary to keep the machine running. This includes courier services and, often, electronic methods of communication such as facsimile transmission.

This usually falls to the lot of the production department to organise since many of the external communications are with suppliers under their control.

In recent years this has become a vital part of the systems of running the magazine as schedules have become faster and more demanding and every stage of the process of getting out the magazine has been shortened.

Advertisement production

An advertisement salesman sells an ad . . . and then the trouble
starts. Getting in copy on time and in the right condition is not
what ad reps are usually good at and if the magazine is big
enough these tasks are often handled by a production person,
whether or not he is part of a central production department.

Much of this is administrative work: keeping track of
schedules for advertisements and chasing up clients or agents
to ensure copy comes in on time. It may also involve monitoring
the total volumes being built up for each issue and informing
those who must decide what size issue to produce.

Assessing the quality of material sent in by agents or clients
for the reproduction of an advertisement is a fairly skilled job
and a very important one if subsequent complaints are to be
avoided. Similarly, checking that all necessary ingredients
have been provided and forwarded to the relevant suppliers
is essential if satisfactory publication is the objective.

The advertisement production man is in the business of
keeping a balance between looking after the needs of clients
who are essential to the financial wellbeing of the magazine
and persuading those who are less than efficient to produce
their text, artwork, orders or whatever at the right time in the
right condition.

In-house typesetting

Technology in magazines, as elsewhere, changes working
practices.

One of the fundamental changes in recent years has been
the development of typesetting systems which can be operated
from within an office environment by journalists rather than
trained typesetters. The magazine industry is approaching
this possibility quite slowly, with only a handful as yet
managing their own typesetting, but the potential is there and

in-house typesetting will in due course become commonplace within the industry.

The Production Department is normally called upon to research and make recommendations about such systems and possibly to implement them.

This requires a degree of detailed knowledge about what the trade calls 'front-end' technology which is rapidly being acquired by many production staff and which is adding a new and interesting dimension to their skills.

The systems themselves range from relatively simple 'desktop publishing' set-ups, running packaged software and available from any computer supplier to highly sophisticated professional typesetting kit built by specialist companies and involving a substantial investment in money and expertise. The appropriate system is determined by the demands of the magazine.

Production flexibility

We have briefly looked at some of the demands made on a typical production department. There may well be others, because production departments are often regarded as useful administrative departments where the staff can turn their hands to most things requiring central control or liaison with other departments.

But the central role remains the timely production of a respectably printed magazine and this becomes ever more challenging as higher and higher standards of professionalism are expected in response to increasing competitive pressure and advancing technological resourcefulness.

Production jobs have become critical and demanding, requiring technical knowledge, numeracy and tact. The status of the production expert has increased significantly in the industry, with higher levels of personal and academic qualification being sought.

It can be a tough but fulfilling job.

If one of the inevitable shortcomings in the production of an issue is the responsibility of a supplier, the production department, as the representative of the supplier, will be at fault by association. But if the systems work well, if the suppliers perform on time and produce good quality work and if a sparkling product is produced, it can be a very exciting and satisfying life.

Market research and sales analysis is an increasingly intellectual activity.

8
Marketing and Promotion

THE FUNCTIONS associated with marketing and promotion vary enormously in different magazine or magazine groups according to the types of periodical being published and the companies' structures. The degree of promotion is also widely different.

On big consumer titles very expensive and elaborate promotion and marketing campaigns are run continuously, with millions of pounds laid out on all forms of media advertising, special events, publicity drives and the like to keep a magazine's image in front of the public. On small business titles marketing effort may be on a more modest scale, centred around mail shots and activity within the trade represented by the magazine.

But most publications need some promotion from time to time if they are to gain sales and grow bigger rather than smaller.

Marketing departments

On *Computing Update* you will note from chapter two we have appointed a Promotions Manager. This is a relatively small magazine compared with, say, a mass-market women's mag, and although it participates in a lively fashion in the events of the computing world and constantly strives to gain extra sales of copies and advertisement space, it does not have a huge budget for these purposes.

The Promotions Manager will use quite a lot of outside help, from other departments in the company, such as the Design Studio, and from external sources, such as mailing houses, in achieving his ends.

On the mass-market women's magazine mentioned above, the scene might be very different, with a large marketing department comprising specialists such as a media buyer, copywriters, a special design facility, and so on, possibly shared with other magazines in the group. On a very small publication such as a learned journal the publisher himself may undertake a modest but steady promotional push, probably using a specialist company to draw up lists of potential subscribers and send them mail shots.

Different publishers approach the challenge in a way which suits their own titles and the structure of their companies, but some activities are common throughout the trade and we will look at these in a fairly random fashion to try to give a flavour of the jobs involved.

Direct mail

Selling anything by direct mail has become quite a science over the past decade or so. As with many business activities, the techniques have been modified by the availability of sophisticated computer hardware and software which can produce detailed sales analysis reports.

Using *Computing Update* as an example, it will be possible for a specialist company to identify all those people employed in the computer world, whether working for manufacturing companies, out in the field as engineers, selling in retail outlets or employed in data processing departments in companies.

Computing Update will want to mail these people to offer subscriptions to the magazine.

Lists of names and addresses can be drawn up, mail shots prepared, and the 'list' mailed selectively with coded response forms so that the percentages of sales resulting from the different sectors identified within the list may be deduced and the results analysed to indicate which parts of the market will respond best to this type of approach. Using these results, the marketing cost per subscription obtained can be worked out and the list possibly further refined to home in on the sectors producing the highest 'response rates'.

That's a relatively straightforward operation; the complications occur when, for example, the Publisher wants to know how many of those who bought subscriptions are likely to renew them the following year. Maybe the cost per subscription sold is too high unless he can be sure a decent percentage will go on to buy another year's worth of the magazine without further mailing.

This information can best be worked out from an analysis of the history of subscription renewals as indicated from statistics taken from the magazine's computer subscription fulfilment system. How many buyers in these market sectors normally do renew their subscriptions and for how many years? In the next chapter we refer again to the need for the order processing system which can give this information to be very carefully specified.

It becomes clear that this type of promotion requires considerable intellectual input if it is to be used productively.

Copywriting

Apart from the business of sales analysis referred to above, it is also obvious that someone must write and prepare the mailshots . . . and this sort of work will recur in the other activities mentioned later.

Copywriting is the term originally used to describe the preparation of text for advertisements but these days it embraces any type of promotional sales literature.

Good copywriting is a considerable skill because it involves the ability to write in a specific rather than a personal style and to write aggressive and dynamic prose which is nevertheless plausible to the reader. A good piece of copywriting reads as though it was written easily and fast but in reality much care goes into this type of work and not everyone can get to grips with the business of slanting text in such a deliberate fashion.

To produce successful work it is first necessary to understand fully the message to be passed on, then to extract the most appealing parts of it and make capital of them. Liaison with the designer is, of course, essential and in many cases the two must work as a team.

This is a valuable talent, much in demand in the marketing world, and those who have it are much sought after.

Advertising

In addition to carrying advertisements, many magazines are themselves advertisers. With large amounts of money at stake in a big marketing campaign, an agency will normally be employed to buy space in the media on behalf of the company or to provide a full service for the campaign. In more modest circumstances, where a few ads are occasionally used in specific circumstances, the magazine may itself undertake the preparation and placing of these.

We saw in chapter five that the analysis of the media and its pulling power is an intricate business so it is enough to point out here that someone, whether a professional media buyer or not, must make a careful study of the most cost-effective means to the end they seek and must then be in a position to prepare or commission suitable material.

Press and public relations

Magazines make news in addition to reporting it and this is excellent publicity if handled well. A magazine leading a campaign or publishing controversial material will attract the attention of other branches of the media and will want to use this publicity productively.

Press releases will be prepared, contacts established with newspapers and television, interviews arranged, briefing sessions organised and – in the case of major campaigns – press receptions and other events staged to gain maximum exposure.

Within the subject areas covered by a magazine there will be constant public relations work to ensure the magazine's profile is kept high in its market. This might range from general discussions with interested individuals and organisations at one end of the scale to lavish presentations and entertainments at the other.

All this involves many different types of work: the maintenance of personal contacts, copywriting, administration and complex organisation.

This side of the business is great fun for those with the energy and a taste for a lively life with sometimes somewhat unsocial hours.

Conferences and exhibitions

Conferences and exhibitions are becoming a regular part of business life and magazines can play both a passive and active role as participants or organisers.

Many magazines attend exhibitions as part of their marketing strategy, seeing this as a method of meeting many of their readers face to face, presenting their magazine's purpose to its market and seeking views and responses.

It often falls to the Promotions Department to book the

space at the show, prepare the stand, staff it and organise literature to be distributed. Anyone who has been involved in this knows the enormous volume of work created by an apparently simple decision to attend!

Many magazines also organise conferences and exhibitions on their own behalf or for other organisations. Although not strictly the subject of this book, it is worth touching on here because in many companies these activities are spasmodic enough to be part of the magazine management's tasks or, where more systematic and concentrated work goes on, the 'conferences division' may fall within the responsibilities of the magazine management.

Staging a conference is an administrative challenge on quite a scale; staging a conference and exhibition requires considerable resources and much time and planning. Again, this is exciting work needing a cool head and bags of energy and enthusiasm combined with the ability to attend scrupulously to all the detail.

Advertisement sales promotion

The business of backing up advertisement sales personnel with promotional materials and activities may come under the aegis of the Advertisement Department or may fall to the lot of the promotions and marketing people but it is an increasingly important function.

As we saw in chapter five, ad space is sold by persuading buyers in a logical fashion that they will get worthwhile results. This needs, in the first place, the analysis to prove the point, and, in the second, the ability to present the facts persuasively.

Literature must be produced. Mailshots must go out. Possibly, promotional events must be arranged.

Often very elaborate and impressive material is produced to back up a magazine's advertisement sales message and much creativity and hard work can go into this.

... and much, much more

We've looked briefly at some of the main functions in marketing and promotions, but of course it does not end there.

The circulation and distribution people need support; competitions may be run; special offers may be made; special services to readers may be organised ... there can be any number of bright ideas limited only by the resources the publication is prepared to commit to promoting itself.

The people needed to do this work can come into the business in many ways: from other departments, as graduate recruits, as marketing people from other companies and other types of commerce. But, as we have seen elsewhere, the quality of staff needed is higher than ever and professionalism is the name of the game.

Much marketing work is specific to the product sold but some requirements are general. The intellect to make intelligent analyses of a market and design sales activity specifically and cost-effectively is vital; the resourcefulness to handle complex administration problems without allowing a panic to develop is necessary; a facility with words and the skill to put over a message in an articulate style is required; and, as ever, the business is about people, inside and outside the organisation, so the natural ability to make good contacts and keep them up is essential.

Persuading the newsagent his customers really need your magazine.

9
Circulation and Distribution

MAGAZINES reach their readers via a retail outlet of some sort (e.g. a bookstall), through the postal system, or, in a few cases, by being handed out in public places such as railway stations or placed in the seat pockets on aeroplanes.

Some are sold and some are free but, even in the case of a 'free sheet', the identification of the market and the requirement to reach the readers the advertiser needs is fundamental to the success of the publication. As with most products, distribution is both a logistical and a marketing exercise. In any sophisticated society, the mechanics of getting a product to its end user are complex enough but to drive this system as a positive marketing vehicle is the real skill.

We will therefore look at both elements – the distribution systems and the use of them as marketing tools – together ... because that is how they are perceived in a magazine company.

Trade distribution

When publishers talk about 'the trade' they mean the newstrade. 'Trade distribution' is therefore the sale of copies through newsagents or CTNs (confectioner, tobacconist, newsagents) as the jargon has it.

The trade divides up broadly into wholesalers and retailers, who take a percentage of the cover price of the magazine as commission.

Why wholesalers? Well, one good reason is that there are about 40,000 retail outlets, so for logistical reasons alone some type of clearing house is necessary.

There are over 200 wholesale houses but in practice a very large chunk of this trade is in the hands of very few companies. W.H. Smith alone account for around 50% of the business and Menzies almost another 25%.

The structure of the *retail* trade, however, is quite different, with about 85% of outlets in independent hands and the multiples only accounting for between 5000-6000 of the shops. Here we see W.H. Smith have but 400 or so of the 40,000 possible outlets. Not all the possible sales outlets are shops in the conventional sense. There are, for example, about 7,000 garage forecourts with CTN stalls of one kind or another.

The need to consolidate distribution through the wholesalers becomes apparent.

The ability of the wholesalers to participate in pro-active marketing has increased significantly in recent years and they now have sophisticated methods of assessing demand, keeping track of sales and regulating subsequent orders. This will further intensify as electronic point of sale systems (EPOS) come into use. EPOS is a method of using bar code readers and other electronic gadgets to keep track of all copies sold and provide automatic analysis of sales patterns, values, stocks, and so on. As yet in its infancy as far as newsagents are concerned, EPOS will in due course become a very powerful tool for regulating orders and supplies.

Both in terms of effective management and marketing skills, newsagents are facing a fairly formidable challenge. When it is considered that nearly 40% of retailers have turnovers of less than £100,000 a year, the difficulty of their keeping pace with new ideas in technology and marketing is obvious and the need for wholesalers to provide an energetic service is critical.

But first the copies must get to them, so let's take a look at the physical systems of distribution.

Distribution to the trade involves a cycle of actions which recur issue by issue and stimulate further actions and reactions. Fig. 2 helps to demonstrate this.

If we take *Computing Update* as an example and begin with the stage in the production process when printed copies start to appear off the end of the binding line, we can return later to this point on the circle and explain how we decided on the print run in the first place.

For the sake of simplicity, we have assumed that *Computing Update* has its own circulation and distribution department which liaises with wholesalers, sends reps out, works out print orders and produces all the necessary documentation to control the distribution. In practice, this is unlikely unless the magazine is part of a large group which shares such facilities among all its magazines; it would be more usual for these functions to be handled by a professional distribution and marketing company (of which there are several) which manages such matters for other companies as well as for its proprietor-magazines. But we'll stick with our simplistic theme to reduce the permutations we have to consider.

The speed at which a magazine can be printed and bound is largely determined by the binding process, which is the last production stage.

Computing Update with its print run of 50,000 will take several hours to bind and, because it is a weekly produced to tight schedules, distribution will occur progressively as the number of finished copies builds up. The Distribution Department will have supplied lists showing how many copies have to go to which wholesalers and will have provided labels to attach to the parcels which will be wrapped up automatically by a machine at the end of the binding line with

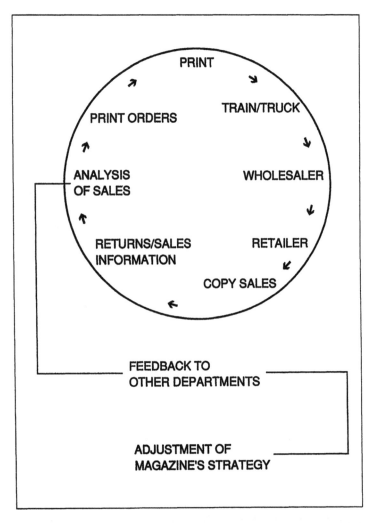

Fig. 2. Distribution to the trade involves a cycle of actions which recur issue by issue and stimulate further actions and reactions. The sales information, when fed back to the magazine's other departments, can be used positively to influence future strategy.

pre-determined numbers of magazines in each parcel. Usually these will be shrink-wrapped with the label sealed inside so that it is clearly visible to all concerned.

Two options are now possible: either vans will take deliveries to the railway terminii where the loads will go by rail to be dropped off at the parcels offices nearest to the wholesalers or the loads will be delivered by road to the wholesalers, possibly consolidated with other magazines.

Rail is fastest but also more expensive (currently about 30% more).

At the wholesalers, parcels are broken down and copies go into 'boxes', which represent the accounts of the individual newsagents, and are then delivered to them.

Sales are monitored by the wholesalers and information is fed back to the publisher. The publisher modifies his future print orders as appropriate and the cycle continues.

Magazines may be offered for sale to the trade in two ways: *firm sale* or *sale and return*. In the first case, the newsagent has placed a firm order for which he carries the financial risk. In the second case, the publisher is effectively allowing the return of unsold copies, which will be credited to the newsagent.

Many market leader magazines do not offer sale or return facilities in the normal course of events but such arrangements are becoming increasingly common and even well-established periodicals may go out on sale or return from time to time as part of a sales promotion exercise. When this happens, the wholesaler will put additional, unordered copies in the newsagents' boxes and this is known in the trade as 'boxing out'.

Throughout the year, but especially during special promotional pushes, reps from the Circulation Department will be visiting wholesalers and retailers, persuading them to take more copies, sharpening up the systems of communication, trying to speed up the flow of information (for it can take up to 90 days before the returns from a sale or return exercise have been cleared) and generally trying to discover whether there is anything they or the magazine can do to sell more copies.

A magazine which is not wanted by readers will ultimately end up with copies left on the newsagents' shelves however good the sales and distribution arrangements, but it is equally true that a good magazine will fail to realise its full sales potential if it is not given every chance of reaching its readership so it is a vital part of the circulation man's job to ensure that it gets maximum exposure in the trade. This involves constant liaison with retailers and wholesalers, feedback of information to the circulation and editorial departments and, from time to time, special promotional pushes to keep the title in the forefront of the customer's field of vision.

This is a job for someone who enjoys contact with customers, is methodical and systematic and has the energy and self-motivation to go out on the road and sell hard. It is a lot of fun but needs considerable drive and stamina.

Subscription sales

Most periodicals have some 'subscribers': buyers who prefer to order copies to be delivered regularly through the post. Some – especially learned journals and very specialised publications – rely mainly on subscription sales.

The management of subscription systems has developed into a fine art as magazines have become aware of the marketing potential of direct mail sales. The great advantage, of course, is that the subscription magazine knows exactly who the customers are: their names, addresses and – if the system has been set up well – a lot of other information as well.

The single most influential factor in the creation of sophisticated subscription management systems has been the availability of fast, inexpensive mini- and microcomputers which can hold large volumes of data, process accounts with a high degree of automation and output mailing labels in a sequence which helps the post office deliver more easily and so attracts a discounted delivery service.

As with trade distribution, the purpose of the exercise is to combine the physical service of delivering copies quickly and effectively with the business of using the system to market the product positively. In the previous chapter, we looked at the possibilities for direct selling by mail and commented that the process of selling to and servicing subscribers feeds on itself: a renewed subscription is as important as a new sale.

The system which handles this must therefore be as good as human ingenuity can devise.

Larger publishers have their own systems, although there are several specialist companies which offer a complete service, holding all a magazine's subscriber details, managing their accounts, outputting mailing labels, producing sales and statistical information about the customers and generally acting as a subscription department.

Even when an outside agency is used, however, there is considerable skill in specifying the magazine's needs in the first place, monitoring the effectiveness of the agency's work and using its facilities imaginatively.

Experience is very valuable here. It is tempting to require every subscriber to fill in a multi-page form which provides masses of information which can then be used by the marketing people but there is a critical level of complexity where the effort required of the potential reader becomes counter-productive. There is also a fine balance between having the selected information presented usefully and having a mass of useless data which requires exhausting analysis and tells the publisher nothing worth knowing.

In the final analysis, the most important criterion for any magazine subscription system is that it gets the magazine to the reader reliably and cost-effectively.

This requires a combination of several skills on the part of those involved.

Firstly, the computer system itself must have been specified to give the publisher what he needs both to handle the subscribers' accounts and to provide information. Do subscribers all take out subscriptions and renew at the same time of the year or must there be a facility to start and renew a subscription at any time of the year? Are all payments cash with order or is a credit facility needed, together with all the chasing stages when recalcitrant subscribers fail to pay up on time? Are some subscriptions handled through intermediate agents who take a commission on the sale and – worse still – are some in foreign currencies which need to be converted at varying rates of exchange? Will some customers be paying on behalf of other customers at different addresses? And so on, with a seemingly endless range of complications and permutations familiar to anyone who has tried to specify such things to a world-weary systems analyst who knows he will only be told a small fraction of the possible horrors implicit in any order processing service.

Secondly, how are the labels to be output? Will the wrapping of the magazines demand a special type of label? Will it go inside the wrapper or outside? Will it be stuck on a 'carrier sheet' which lies on top of the magazine, stuck on the film wrapping, or what? What order must they be in when output? If the publisher is to take advantage of special rates negotiated with the Post Office for magazine distribution, then the labels must be sorted into a special sequence which avoids some of the usual subsequent sortation by the postal service.

Thirdly, the physical distribution must be managed. How are the magazines to be wrapped: envelopes, shrink wrapping, or what? What weight of wrapping material is necessary to ensure safe delivery but keep costs to a minimum? How long will the wrapping and labelling take after the magazines have been delivered from the binding line?

And what of overseas sales? What methods of air freight or

combinations of sea, air and land can be used to get copies to
eager readers in India or Australia?

The logistics are complex and fascinating, substantial costs
are involved and there is ample opportunity to apply a keen
intellect to devising intelligent schemes which are efficient
and economic.

'The competition for top jobs is fierce.'

10

The Management

IN EARLIER CHAPTERS we have looked at the roles of the Editor and departmental managers, so here we are concerned primarily with those at board level or thereabouts, how their careers developed to such elevated positions and how they spend their time.

The boards of publishing companies, like most other enterprises, tend to comprise a chairman, a managing director or chief executive and divisional directors responsible for subsidiary companies or for discrete parts of the operation. Interestingly, there is no discernable pattern in the career paths followed by the chairmen and managing directors of magazine publishers other than that most of them came out of the industry rather than a business college.

Some came up along an editorial route, some were marketing people, some had pursued other specialisms.

The only common factor, which may be inferred rather than demonstrated, is that at some stage in their lives they began to take a close interest in the broader business side of the organisation: the financial performance and the overall management of the company.

The potential to develop such curiosity is more or less permanently present in all parts of a magazine operation since, as we have seen, all departments must liaise with each other, are constantly in discussion about the economic implications of their activities and are continuously reminded of the periodical's business strategy. However, it is by no means predetermined that all staff will aspire to participate in such matters at the top level.

A good journalist is not necessarily a good businessman. He may not want to be a businessman; after all, he has highly respectable skills of his own and faces challenges which are quite absorbing enough as he practises his craft. The same is true of other staff and some have no management ambitions.

Nevertheless, it is patently obvious to all those who work on a magazine that the task of directing the development of such an interesting and volatile business is very exciting indeed and many are called to have a go at the top jobs.

Many are called . . . but few are chosen. The competition for top jobs in publishing is fierce and judgment is largely given on the basis of achievement and track record. It is usually necessary, therefore, that the high flier be particularly talented as well as hard working. He must also have outstanding personal qualities for he must manage a team of highly intelligent staff (we hope) and a fast-running machine which demands constant attention.

But because most senior managers have come up through the trade, albeit with professional training en route, the opportunity to get to the top is there for every member of staff.

Let's look at some of the responsibilities which go along with the top jobs.

Strategic planning

All companies, whatever their businesses and however well or badly run, have a strategic plan. It is true that in the case of a very small company, this may be unwitting and comprise an instinctive wish to go about a business in the only way the proprietor knows how, taking advantage of any opportunities which may occur along the way . . . but even this is a strategy of sorts. Also, in the case of a newly-launched, small magazine – the 'wish and a prayer' publication mentioned in our opening chapter – the strategy may simply embrace a passionate belief that there is a market for a certain type of magazine and a knowledge of the critical path which must be followed to take advantage of it. That is also a broad strategy of sorts.

But a company of any size needs a somewhat more sophisticated set of plans and aspirations, firstly because its business is more complicated and its options are more numerous and secondly because, as the number of staff employed increases, so does the requirement to ensure that all the oarsmen in the boat are rowing in the same direction, that all the staff understand what the company is trying to achieve and the steps which are being taken to attain that goal. This demands a set of objectives which are more than a gleam in the chairman's eye: objectives which have been clearly defined, understood and agreed by the senior management; objectives for which the necessary resources have been allocated; objectives which have consequences implicit in the working routines, business and publishing targets of all the staff.

Defining a strategy and communicating it throughout the organisation is therefore one of the prime responsibilities of senior management.

At its broadest, such a plan can consist of a single, sweeping statement such as:

'We want to consolidate the success of our existing magazines, ensure their position as market leaders and maximise their profit.'

Or:

'We want to diversify our publishing by the acquisition and development of titles in areas of publishing in which we are not presently engaged so as to reduce our vulnerability to the volatility of our present markets.'

Such statements of intent, usually embroidered with some appropriate city jargon, might be found in the Chairmen's Notes in any clutch of annual reports issued by large magazine publishers. Each would be a valid strategy for a company with certain publishing assets and resources at a given stage of its development or in a given financial or publishing environment but each clearly has widely differing implications for the forthcoming months or years of endeavour of its management and staff.

To take our first statement, no new magazines will be bought or launched and all the energies and skills of the staff will be centred on maximising the sales of their current publications. There will be special promotions; concentrated discussions about increasing the appeal of the content; hard work by the circulation department reps to ensure that copies are unfailingly on sale in the right place at the right time in the right numbers; possibly a big sale or return exercise to get circulation up; maybe special issues with regional or special-interest supplements; increased spend on marketing materials; some extra public relations work by the editors out in the field; consideration of peripheral sales to allied market sectors; thoughts about overseas editions if appropriate; costings from the production department on the financial implications of extra pages or more colour; and so on.

In the second scenario, the new activity of the company will be quite different. Research will be conducted into other sectors of the magazine market and the publications which dominate them and high-level contact will be made with their management with a view to acquisition. In the case of new launches, detailed plans will be made through all departments to get the new magazines off the ground. With both new acquisitions and new launches there will be implications for the number of staff employed, how they are to be accommodated, how the administration of the company will handle the extra burden, and so on. Also there will be the question of the cash needed to finance this expansion: how it is to be raised, how much additional cash will be necessary and when. Forecasts of all sorts will be made and re-made to ensure that as far as possible the consequences of this brave new strategy are understood . . . and understood to be desirable.

When the launches happen or the new titles are bought, then of course there will be more frenetic activity as they begin their lives within the company.

Meanwhile, the previous business of the company must go on and must be managed effectively to continue to produce the profits which, in part at least, will have financed the expansion.

Large structures

Some companies have many industrial and commercial interests of which publishing is one, and in these cases the first line of strategy may simply be a decision that magazine publishing is a good business to be in.

Fig. 3 shows a hypothetical structure of a large multi-national corporation owning companies in several different industries and indicating how the responsibilities for management are devolved. Although there is no single text-book version of such arrangements, the dotted line represents a unit of management which is most likely to be the structure recognisable to a member of staff working within it and within which the strategy which affects his job will be devised and implemented.

Deciding broad strategic plans within this structure is usually the role of the Chairman or Managing Director in consultation with his masters and his own senior management. The task requires a mixture of entrepreneurial flair and business experience plus a knowledge of the marketplace. Implementing the consequences of the plan is likely to fall, in the first instance, on directors or managers with line

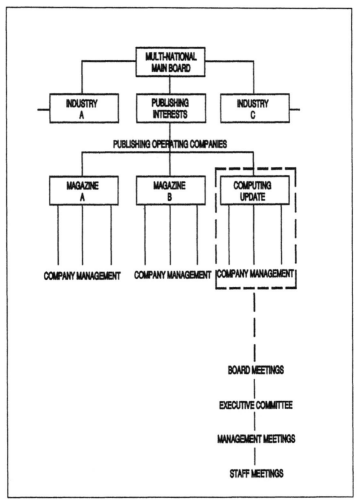

Fig. 3: large structures. Some publishing companies are part of larger groups which have other trading interests. This diagram shows the typical structure of such a group and the sort of meetings which the individual publishing company might use to manage its communications.

responsibility for certain areas of the company.

Special responsibilities

All directors and senior managers in a company have responsibility for contributing to the overall picture and will spend many hours discussing the direction the company should take and the various options open to it. But in most cases they will have particular line management responsibilities which will fill the greater part of their days.

The sizes of units within a management structure can be very different so it is impossible to generalise about precise responsibilities but most senior managers face the same challenges: to develop and motivate their staff in such a way that the unit is at its most creative in performing its part in the publishing system and to use their own experience, skills and initiative to interpret the company's strategy as energetically and imaginatively as possible.

Much of their time will be spent on the technicalities of their work, whether it is editorial, advertising, circulation, production or whatever; but much will also be spent managing staff, and the importance of this is worth emphasising.

Most magazine publishers have only two principal assets: their magazines and their staff. Unlike a manufacturing industry, there are no machines which can make or break the company; there is no succession of really dramatic new technologies which will change the nature of the business year by year. The company will succeed or fail depending on the skills of the staff in putting together magazines which the readers want to read and the advertisers want to use. Selecting, developing, motivating and managing those staff effectively is therefore crucial to the success of the company.

There may well be a personnel department which can sort out the administrative detail of 'human resources' (as it is now sometimes called) and which can concentrate the managers' minds on some of the issues to be considered in good staff management. For example, some companies have introduced 'appraisal schemes' whereby managers are required to meet formally with each member of staff at least once a year and discuss progress, ambitions, weaknesses, training needs, and so on, and record both the manager's and the staff member's observations and set targets for future achievement.

Schemes like this are helpful in ensuring that the need for a proper dialogue is not overlooked, but at the end of the long, hard day it will have been the *consistent* effectiveness of the manager's staff relations which will have made most difference to the department's enthusiasm and performance.

In considering a career in magazines, therefore, it is well to remember that those who aspire to line management jobs must have the personal resources to handle the very demanding (and rewarding) business of motivating other people.

Communication

One of the essential elements in good staff management is communication.

Remembering to communicate is the first step, deciding how to is the next.

In a large, busy organisation it is sometimes easy for the manager to forget that he knows things others do not and his staff are building up information which he does not possess. Some of this knowledge would be superfluous to the staff or the manager but some is critical and must be passed on. Often this happens automatically as the working day progresses, especially in small departments where everyone is in close contact most of the time but some needs systems of communication if it is to be properly distributed.

In a large company, regular meetings will necessarily be

part of this system and the ability to hold or participate in meetings is as important as in any other industry. Thinking through problems and opportunities before the meeting takes place; having the necessary documentation prepared in advance; reporting accurately and concisely on his own areas of the business; presenting ideas and plans quickly and with the correct amount of detail; understanding how to prepare and use agendas, minutes and management information: these are skills which must be acquired if the manager is to use his own time well and avoid wasting the time of other managers.

Fig. 3 shows a typical series of meetings which may take place at regular intervals in a large company. The board meeting will discuss strategy and general performance; there may be an executive committee of the board (sometimes called a 'finance committee' or 'management board') to take the implementation business plans to the first stage; management meetings will keep managers in touch with each other's activities and assess their progress towards achieving the company's targets; staff meetings may be held to inform the staff of the general progress of the company and listen to their views.

Managing change

We have noted several times that magazine publishing is a volatile business.

Changes in the tactics necessary to implement a strategy will therefore occur from time to time as a magazine learns more about its market, discovers new ways of interesting readers or pleasing advertisers and adjusts its activities to meet changing fashions or changes in its market.

Sometimes, also, things go wrong and policies fail. Then things must be adjusted.

The change or failure may be quite discrete, such as failing to meet targeted levels of advertising revenue due to a lack of really vigorous salesmanship or may be fundamental, such as the realisation that a newly-launched magazine will not succeed.

This is the most testing time for a manager.

This is where he will discover that all the objectives and targets set for his staff at their 'appraisal interviews' mentioned above have changed and a new set of priorities has taken their place. Sometimes tough decisions will need to be taken as retrenchment occurs in areas of the business.

It is crucial in these circumstances that a manager is sufficiently well-respected by his staff for his interpretation of events to be believed, understood and accepted and strong and resourceful enough to steer his department onto a new course.

Strength of purpose is therefore another essential quality for the aspiring manager.

Acquiring skills

We have looked at the role of magazine management, considered some of the special responsibilities shouldered, and mentioned some essential qualities and skills needed.

It is a potentially daunting prospect if the responsibilities and skills are listed without a further qualification: that much of the ability to manage is acquired through the practice of the craft and the development of experience and that the possibilities for this within a magazine publishing environment are excellent.

It is also necessary to point out that much effort is being devoted to training professional management and that bodies like the Periodicals Training Council are ensuring that a new generation of professional managers is appearing. In chapter 11 we note the type of courses available but we should make the point now that this emphasis on professionalism has encouraging implications both for graduates with management qualifications, whose special attainments will be recognised, and for those uninitiated in the mysteries of running a business who can be confident that appropriate training is now available.

It has been said that in magazine publishing there are no careers – there are simply opportunities to be taken. This is an over-simplification of an industry which does actually have some sort of career structure, but there is an element of truth in it.

There are no effective barriers to progress through to the top of a magazine publishing company other than the qualities of the aspirants and the qualities of those already there. In an expanding industry, this is an exciting prospect for those with ambitions to fly high and it is one of the great attractions of the industry.

'Aims to prepare the all-round journalist.'

11
Training

ATTITUDES TO TRAINING within the magazine publishing industry have changed significantly in recent years.

Not so long ago it was the conventional wisdom that the only training really worth having was 'on the job'. It was relatively recently that the realisation dawned that learning through a painful process of making mistakes was expensive, disruptive and probably largely unnecessary. Learning processes based on trial and error have an unfortunate tendency to lead to a rash of mistakes and editorial solecisms which may entertain readers but do little to keep down editors' blood pressures.

Past, present and future

The provincial newspaper industry initially led the way to a more structured approach by introducing the National Council for the Training of Journalists Proficiency Certificate: a qualification which covered a range of subjects appropriate to building the skills of a newspaper journalist and which could be obtained through part-time or block-release study.

Magazines, which nowadays draw on the provincial press for only a small percentage of their editorial staff, were slower to adopt formal schemes for their own industry but have gradually developed a more considered approach which will shortly be further refined by a government commitment to 'vocational qualification'.

An earlier government had introduced the Printing and Publishing Industry Training Board (now disbanded) which funded training on a 'levy/grant' basis, compulsory for all large companies which could not demonstrate they had adequate resources of their own. This had several weaknesses, including the propensity of the more cynical companies to spend more effort on making out a case for exemption than on joining in on training initiatives.

The present administration, through the National Council for Vocational Training, has called for standards of vocational competence for all occupations. The government also wants sectors to consider a framework of national vocational qualifications (NVQs) based on the accepted standards. Although this has not become a statutory obligation, it is likely to be pursued quite vigorously.

The Periodicals Training Council

In the magazine sector, the challenge has been taken up by the Periodicals Training Council (PTC). The PTC was set up in 1982 after the abolition of the Printing and Publishing Industry Training Board. It has in membership all major companies and the majority of medium and smaller publishers. It is estimated that almost 90% of the workforce are in membership and it is recognised by the Training Agency as the non-statutory training organisation for periodical publishing. The PTC has researched the ground to be covered by a vocational qualification and suitable methods of providing instruction and monitoring progress and will be the examining body for periodical journalism.

Meanwhile, it initiates and co-ordinates most existing training activities. These range from one-day seminars to full-scale courses supported by government funding and include on-the-job and distance learning schemes.

The courses cover editorial, management, new technology, production and advertisement sales.

Editorial training

The Editorial Training Scheme is the most ambitious of the PTC's programmes. It lays down ground to be covered to give the trainee the necessary knowledge and skill to become proficient in the essential editorial disciplines. It must be completed in a period of not more than three and not less than two years.

To assist both tutor and trainee, progress is monitored using an *Editorial Training Log* which records the training followed and the trainee's achievements. The training is divided into four areas:

news writing

feature writing

subbing

layout and design

These will form the basis of the NVQ in the 1990s.

Detailed lists of subjects to be covered are included within each section and there are further 'training suggestions' which promote extra exercises, attendances at specific meetings, visits to technical suppliers, additional specialist instruction, and so on.

How much of this goes on depends somewhat on the enthusiasm of the trainee's company for extending his experience, his own curiosity to broaden his knowledge and the stamina of the executive responsible for his journalistic evolution, but it is also conditioned by the amount of 'live' work the journalist is undertaking. It is one of the most frustrating paradoxes of all forms of on-the-job training that the most talented trainees tend to get the least training opportunities since they are more immediately pressed into active service and time for further education becomes scarce.

The editorial log helps control this tendency but probably cannot completely prevent it.

As the requirements of the log are achieved, so each section is signed off by the shaking hand of the trainee's tutor.

A substantial *Guide to Editorial Practice* provides documentary support and there is a range of external courses, including a full-time block-release course (in two two-week sections) at the London College of Printing, covering:

interviewing and reporting

writing copy: news and features

editing copy and preparing it for the printer

understanding the printing process

layout and design

law for journalists: libel, copyright, consumer law, etc

how the industry is organised and the journalist's role in industry and society

As mentioned in chapter two, some journalists arrive in their first job having already undertaken basic training.

The PTC approves and monitors the following centres for pre-entry editorial training:

City University, London

University College, Cardiff

London College of Printing

Reed Business Publishing

Journalism courses have been running at City University since 1976 and the Graduate Centre for Journalism is now established as a full department of the University.

Since it is situated in London, the Centre can call on the industry to help make the journalism education it provides relevant and can keep in touch with latest developments.

The Centre runs a one-year diploma course in periodical journalism which has a strong vocational orientation. All the permanent teaching staff are former full-time journalists who maintain their working contacts with the industry. The teaching is also supplemented heavily by contributions from working journalists.

The course runs from late September until the beginning of July. About 40 students are enrolled and working attachments on periodicals are arranged.

The magazine option at the Centre for Journalism Studies in Cardiff became available in 1985 and aims to 'prepare the all-round journalist'. This includes reporting and writing news, writing features and the full production cycle of sub editing, layout and page design. The college describes it as a 'broad and demanding syllabus which calls for commitment and application'.

Class work and assignments are brought together when the students produce their own magazine, for which they write the copy, design pages and typeset the text on the Centre's direct input system. Editorial submissions by students to the press are also encouraged and magazine attachments are arranged over the Easter vacation.

The London College of Printing offers one-year and two-year full-time pre-entry course for school leavers with A level qualifications. The curriculum includes:

Editorial practice: research, interviewing, reporting, feature writing, sub editing copy, use of pictures, production methods, basic editorial typography and layout, proof reading.

Editorial office skills: typing and presentation of copy, wordprocessing and computer typesetting.

Related subjects: advanced editorial assignment (choice of one of five specialised options), appreciation of printing processes, principles of law for journalists, contemporary affairs, communications industry/media analysis, and shorthand to a speed of 100 words a minute.

Reed Business Publishing's course is basically designed for their own intake of staff but is also open to outside entrants. The PTC can advise further on the suitability of all these opportunities.

All the pre-entry courses have limited intakes so competition is fierce.

Further basic training should be unnecessary for journalists completing pre-entry courses although most will need some extra training in specifics during the settling-in period to a first job.

Addresses of the Colleges running pre-entry courses are given in Appendix 2.

Management training

For managers the PTC currently runs two courses: one for the business press and one for the consumer press. These are fully residential and are aimed at the publisher – the person who has or will have overall management responsibility for the publishing operation and who needs help with aspects of the business on the commercial side.

Experts at the top levels in publishing companies contribute to sessions which cover all aspects of publishing: marketing, editorial, advertising, circulation, production and finance. Delegates work in syndicates to tackle detailed case studies and present their solution to a panel of publishing specialists for assessment and comment.

Short courses deal with typesetting technology, including the in-house use of editing terminals. The courses are run at Watford College, which has a wide selection of equipment for hands-on use and comparison and analysis. One course is aimed at managers, the other at editorial staff. Both are essentially practical in nature.

Production training

A distance-learning scheme – also prepared by Watford College – is available to production staff. Logically divided into modules which roughly equate to the various production processes, the course is intended to take the trainee through the technical side of periodicals publishing at a measured pace. The modules include:

the publishing industry

printing processes

typesetting

graphic reproduction

machine printing

finishing and binding

There are, incidentally, editorial, advertisement production and law units also available under this distance learning scheme.

Advertisement sales training

The PTC's advertisement sales training programme comprises courses which concentrate on sales tactics and techniques.

Course titles include:

Preparation and planning – defining the client's needs

Face-to-face presentation skills

Objections – how to overcome them

Selling against the competition

Staying with the rate card – negotiation and closing

Telephone selling techniques

An advertisement sales training log, similar in concept to the editorial log, is also produced by the PTC.

Publishers' training schemes

Some of the bigger publishing companies run their own independent training schemes. These vary considerably in style, content and overall structure. Some are specifically editorial; others are designed to develop future senior managers. Benn, Morgan Grampian and Haymarket are examples of companies which have well-developed systems in place.

Ads addressed to future graduates are often placed around Easter time in the national press.

Written applications are assessed and candidates asked for interview. Qualities looked for include good academic performance although the training staff stress that they are at least as interested in:

a bright mind

mental agility: the ability to argue a case well

strong interpersonal skills

attention to detail (mistakes in cvs and applications do not improve the probability of employment) good spelling (boring but necessary, at least for sub editors!)

enthusiasm

any evidence that the candidate can write reasonably fluently

There is usually a formal training period but much time is spent in on-the-job activities. Most of the classroom training is handled by internal staff although specialists are drafted in where necessary, e.g. to cover the arcane working of the libel laws.

After completion of the training period, journalists are 'placed' on one of the company's magazines, either to occupy a specific vacancy or in a supernumerary capacity until a vacancy arises.

Other organisations

Other organisations central to or on the periphery of magazine publishing also provide training.

The Periodical Publishers Association arranges frequent seminars at all levels on a variety of subjects.

Some are broad considerations of topical aspects of the industry designed to keep members aware of changing circumstances, matters needing urgent attention, or explanations of PPA activities undertaken on behalf of members.

Others are specifically targeted training in technical areas. On the production side, for example, the PPA's Production Committee recently initiated courses adapted from material originally developed by Reed Business Publishing in collaboration with the Printing Industries Research Association and produced useful two-day and one-day units on *Printing and Finishing Techniques, Graphic Reproduction* and *Litho Printing*.

The Printing Industries Research Association itself runs an extensive series of courses and seminars on production-related issues ranging from introductory sessions on the principles of print production to highly detailed expositions of complex processes unintelligible to all but the dedicated expert.

The British Printing Industries Federation (BPIF) (which represents printers rather than publishers) believes it has a responsibility to develop proper standards of communication between periodical printers and publishers and puts some considerable effort into arranging regular sessions which consider aspects of liaison between the two sides and the development of professional procedures.

Then there are independent but active specialist training organisations offering a good set of occasional options.

In all, recent years have seen the establishment of a decent fund of training resources generated within the industry and externally and a healthily balanced attitude towards training on the part of most of the leading magazine publishers. The advent of a vocational training qualification should complete the picture.

Members of the Periodical Publishers Association

ABDP, CBD Research Ltd.
15 Wickham Road, Beckenham, Kent BR3 2JS

A E Morgan Publications Ltd
Stanley House, 9 West Street, Epsom KT18 7RL

AGB Business Publications Ltd
Audit House, Field End Road, Eastcote, Ruislip HA4 9LT

AGB Heighway Publications Ltd
Cloister Court, 22-26 Farringdon Lane, London EC1R 3AU

AGB Hulton Ltd
Warwick House, Azalea Drive, Swanley BR8 8JF

AGB Specialist Publications Ltd
Audit House, Field End Road, Eastcote, Ruislip HA4 9LT

AIM Publications Ltd
Silver House, 31-35 Beak Street, London W1R 3LD

Ambassador Publishing
Elstree House, Elstree Way, Borehamwood, Herts WD6 1LU

Angel Publishing Ltd
Kingsland House, 361-373 City Road, London EC1V 1LR

Argus Business Publications Ltd
Queensway House, 2 Queensway, Redhill, Surrey RH1 1QS

Argus Consumer Publications Ltd
Victory House, Leicester Place, London WC2H 7NB

Argus Health Publications Ltd
Victory House, Leicester Place, London WC2H 7NB

Argus Press Ltd
Queensway House, 2 Queensway, Redhill, Surrey RH1 1QS

Argus Specialist Publications Ltd
Argus House, Boundary Way, Hemel Hempstead, HP2 7ST

Batiste Publications Ltd
Pembroke House, Campsbourne Road, London N8 7PE

Barker Publications Ltd
Barker House, 539 London Road, Isleworth TW7 4DA

BBC Magazines
35 Marylebone High Street, London W1M 4AA

BEAP Ltd
Glenthorne House, Hammersmith Grove, London W6 OLG

Benn Publications Ltd
Sovereign Way, Tonbridge, Kent TN9 1RW

Brand Publishing Ltd
47 Dartford Road, Sevenoaks, Kent TN13 3TE

British Tourist Authority
Thames Tower, Black's Road, London W6 9EL

Brown Knight and Truscott Ltd
Local Government Chronicle, 122 Minories, London EC3N 1NT

Burlington Publishing Co Ltd
10 Sheet Street, Windsor, Berks SL4 1BG

Butterick Co Ltd
New Lane, Havant, Hants PO9 2ND

Carson & Comerford Ltd
Stage House, 47 Bermondsey Street, London SE1 3XT

Centaur Communications Ltd
49-50 Poland Street, London W1B 4AX

Conde Nast Publications Ltd
Vogue House, Hanover Square, London W1R OAD

Croner Publications Ltd
Croner House, London Road, Kingston-upon-Thames,

Surrey KT2 6SR

D C Thomson & Co Ltd
Courier Buildings, Dundee, Scotland DD1 9QJ

Director Publications Ltd
Mountbarrow House, Elizabeth Street, London SW1W 9RB

Dog World Ltd
9 Tufton Street, Ashford, Kent TN23 1QN

Dominion Press Ltd
Signal House, 16 Lyon Road, Harrow, Middx HA1 2QE

EMAP Plc
1 Lincoln Court, Lincoln Road, Peterborough PE1 2RF

EMAP Maclaren Ltd
PO Box 109, Maclaren House, Scarbrook Road, Croydon CR9
1QH

Encounter Ltd
44 Great Windmill Street, London W1V 7PA

Farming Press Ltd
Wharfedale Road, Ipswich, IP1 4LG

Findlay Publications Ltd
Franks Hall, Horton Kirby, Kent DA4 9LL

Fredericks Communications Plc
3 Stratford Office Village, 4 Romford Way, London E15 4EA

Gainsborough Publishing Ltd
71 Newcomen Street, London SE1 1YT

General Gramophone Pubs Ltd
177-179 Kenton Road, Harrow, Middx HA3 0HA

G J Palmer & Sons Ltd
7 Portugal Street, London WC2A 2HP

Golf World Ltd
Advance House, 37 Mill Harbour, Isle of Dogs, London E14
9TX

Gruner & Jahr (UK)
New Oxford House, 137 High Holborn, London WC1V 6PW

Hachette Magazines Ltd
Rex House, 4-12 Lower Regent Street, London SW1Y 4PE

Hanover Press Ltd
80 Highgate Road, London NW5 1PB

Harmsworth Press Ltd
Magazine Division, Associated Newspapers Group Plc, Carmelite House, London EC4Y OJA

Harrington Kilbride & Partners Ltd
21 Cross Street, Islington, London N1 2BH

Haymarket Publishing Ltd
38-42 Hampton Road, Teddington, Middx TW11 OJE

Heating & Ventilating Pubs Ltd
Faversham House, 111 St James's Road, Croydon CR9 2TH

Hello Ltd
44a Floral Street, Covent Garden, London WC2E 9DA

House Builder Publications Ltd
82 New Cavendish Street, London W1M 8AD

IBC Plc,
57-61 Mortimer Street, London W1N 7ED

ICB Publications Ltd
39-41 North Road, London N7 9DP

IPC Magazines Ltd
SEAL Group, Kings Reach Tower, Stamford Street, London SE1 9LS

ITV Publications Ltd
247 Tottenham Court Road, London W1P OAU

Illustrated London News
91-93 Southwark Street, London SE1 OHX

Industrial Media Ltd
Blair House, High Street, Tonbridge, Ken TN9 1BR

Industrial Trade Journals Ltd
Stakes House, Quebec Square, Westerham, Kent TN16 ITD

International Thomson Publishing Ltd
Business Magazines Division, 100 Avenue Road, Swiss Cottage,
London NW3 3TP

International Thomson Publishing Ltd
First Floor, The Quadrangle, 180 Wardour Street, London W1A
4YG

Jazz Journal Ltd
113-117 Farringdon Road, London EC1R 3BT

Johnsons of Bath
James Street West, Green Park, Bath BA1 2BU

Link House Publications Plc
Link House, West Street, Poole BH15 1LL

Listener Publications Ltd
199-201 Old Marylebone Road, London NW1 5QS

Lloyds of London Press Ltd
Sheepen Place, Colchester, Essex CO3 3LP

Lockwood P
430-438 Market Towers, New Covent Garden Market, London
SW8 5NN

Machinery Market Ltd
6 Blyth Road, Bromley, Kent BR1 3RX

Macmillan Magazines Ltd
4 Little Essex Street, London WC2R 3LF

Maclean Hunter Ltd
Maclean Hunter House, Chalk Lane, Cockfosters Road, Barnet
EN4 OBU

Magnum Publications Ltd
110-112 Station Road East, Oxted, Surrey RH8 OQA

Marathon Videotex Ltd
Queens House, 2 Holly Road, Twickenham, Middx TW1 4EG

Maritime World Ltd
114 South Street, Dorking, Surrey RH4 2EZ

Medical News Tribune Ltd,
Tower House, Southampton Street, London WC2E 7LS

Metal Bulletin Plc
Park House, Park Terrace, Worcester Park, KT4 7HY

Mining Journal Ltd
60 Worship Street, London EC2A 2HD

Morgan Grampian Plc
Morgan Grampian House, 30 Calderwood Street, Woolwich, London SE18 6QH

Murdoch Magazines
King's House, 8-10 Haymarket, London SW1Y 4BP

National Federation of Fish Friers
Federation House, 289 Dewsbury Road, Leeds LS11 5HW

National Magazines Co Ltd
National Magazine House, 72 Broadwick Street, London W1V 2BP

News International-Hachette Ltd
King's House, 8-10 Haymarket, London SW1Y 4BP

Newsweek Inc
Newsweek House, Wellington Street, Slough, Berks SL1 1UG

Paul Cave Publications Ltd,
74 Bedford Place, Southampton, SO1 2DF

Perry Publications Ltd
388-396 Oxford Street, London W1N 9HE

Personnel Publications Ltd
57 Mortimer Street, London W1N 7TD

PPG Publishing Ltd
Kelsey House, 77 High Street, Beckenham, Kent BR3 1AN

Peter Peregrinus Ltd
PO Box 8, Southgate House, Stevenage, SG1 1HG

Peterson Publishing Co Ltd
Peterson House, Northbank, Berryhill Industrial Estate, Droitwich, Worcs WR9 9BL

Plus, Hamfield Publications Ltd
Featherstone Street, London EC1Y 8SL

Police Review Publishing Co Ltd
14 St Cross Street, London EC1N 8FE

Polystyle Publications Ltd
159-161 Camden High Street, London NW1 7JH

Publisher Marketing Services Ltd
42 Grays Inn Road, London WC1X 8LR

Reader's Digest Association Ltd
25 Berkeley Square, London W1X 6AB

Redwood Publishing Ltd
20-26 Brunswick Place, London N1 6DJ

Reed Business Publishing
Quadrant House, The Quadrant, Sutton, Surrey SM2 5AS

RSPB
The Lodge, Sandy, Beds SG19 2DL

Royal Society of Chemistry
Burlington House, Piccadilly, London W1V OBN

Saga Publishing Ltd
25-28 Buckingham Gate, London SW1E 6LD

Scholastic Publications Ltd
Marlborough House, Holly Walk, Leamington Spa, CV32 4LS

Seymour
Windsor House, 1270 London Road, Norbury, London SW16 4DH

Shropshire Publications Ltd
Shropshire House, Capper Street, London WC1E 6JA

Southern Magazines Ltd
Wickham House, 15 The Square, Lenham, Maidstone, Kent

ME17 2PH

Sporting Magazine Publishers Ltd
20 Mount Ash Road, Sydenham, London SE26 6LZ

Statesman & Nation Publishing Co Ltd
Foundation House, Perseverance Works, 38 Kingsland Road, London E2 8BA

Stonehart Leisure Magazines Ltd
62-71 Goswell Road, London EC1V 7EN

Techpress Publishing Co Ltd
Northside House, 69 Tweedy Road, Bromley, Kent BR1 3WA

The Builder Group Plc
Builder House, 1 Millharbour, London E14 9RA

The Economist Newspaper Ltd
25 St. James's Street, London SW1A 1HG

The Lady
39-40 Bedford Street, London WC2E 9ER

The Lancet Ltd
46 Bedford Square, London WC1B 3SL

The Law Society
114 Chancery Lane, London WC2 1PL

The Municipal Group Ltd
178-202 Great Portland Street, London W1N 6NH

The National Trust
36 Queen Anne's Gate, London SW1

The Spectator
56 Doughty Street, London WC1N 2LL

The Tablet Publishing Co Ltd
48 Great Peter Street, London SW1P 2HB

The Times Supplements
Priory House, St John's Lane, London EC1M 4BX

The White Fathers
129 Lichfield Road, Sutton Coldfield, West Midlands, B74 2SA

Thomas Telford Ltd
Thomas Telford House, No 1 Heron Quay, Isle of Dogs, London E14 9XF

Time Out Ltd
Tower House, Southampton Street, London WC2E 7HD

United Newspapers Plc
Ludgate House, 245 Blackfriars Road, London SE1 9UY

Update-Siebert Publications Ltd
Friary Court, 13-21 High Street, Guildford, Surrey GU1 3XD

VNU Business Publications
32-34 Broadwick Street, London W1A 2HG

Weald of Kent Publications Ltd
47 High Street, Tonbridge, Kent TN9 1SD

Whitehall Press Ltd
Earl House, Earl Street, Maidstone, Kent ME14 1PE

William Reed Ltd
5-7 Southwark Street, London SE1 1RQ

Wolters Kluwer Group
Avenue House, 131-133 Holland Park Avenue, London W11 4UT

Wordsearch T/A Blueprint
26 Cramer Street, London W1M 3HE

Useful addresses

Organisations

Advertising Association
Abford House, 15 Wilton Road, London SW1V 1NJ. Tel: 01-828 2771.
Advertising Standards Authority
Brook House, 2-16 Torrington Place, London WC1E 7HN. Tel: 01-580 5555.
Article Number Association (UK) Ltd
6 Catherine Street, London WC2B 5JJ. Tel: 01-836 2460.
Aslib (Association of Special Libraries and Information Bureaux)
3 Belgrave Square, London SW1X 8PL. Tel: 01-235 5050.
Association of Subscription Agents
c/o Blackwells Periodicals Division, PO Box 40, Hythe Bridge Street, Oxford OX1 2EU. Tel: (0865) 792792
British Association of Picture Libraries and Agencies (BAPLA)
PO Box 284, London
British Copyright Council
Copyright House, 29-33 Berners Street, London W1P 3DB. Tel: 01-580 5544.
British Direct Marketing Association (BDMA)
1 New Oxford Street, London WC1A 1NQ. Tel: 01-242 2254.
British Library
2 Sheraton Street, London W1V 4BH. Tel: 01-636 1544.
British Printing Industries Federation (BPIF)
11 Bedford Row, London WC1R 4DX. Tel: 01-242 6904.
British Standards Institution (BSI)
2 Park Street, London W1A 2BS. Tel: 01-629 9000.
City & Guilds of London Institute
76 Portland Place, London W1N 4AA. Tel: 01-580 3050.
Design Council
28 Haymarket, London SW1Y 4SU. Tel: 01-839 8000.

Incorporated Society of British Advertisers Ltd
  44 Hertford Street, London W1Y 8AE. Tel: 01-499 7502.
Institute of Journalists (IOJ)
  Bedford Chambers, Covent Garden, London WC2E 8HA. Tel: 01-836 6541.
Institute of Practitioners in Advertising (IPA)
  44 Belgrave Square, London SW1X 8QS. Tel: 01-235 7020.
International Federation of the Periodical Press Ltd
  Suite 19, Grosvenor Gardens House, 35-37 Grosvenor Gardens, London SW1W 0BS. Tel: 01-828 1366.
National Union of Journalists (NUJ)
  Acorn House, 314 Gray's Inn Road, London WC1X 8PD. Tel: 01-278 7916.
Periodical Barcoding Association
  Imperial House, 15-19 Kingsway, London WC2B 6UN. Tel: 01-379 6268.
Periodical Publishers Association Ltd (PPA)
  Imperial House, 15-19 Kingsway, London WC2B 6UN. Tel 01-379 6268.
PIRA (Printing Industries Research Association)
  Randalls Road, Leatherhead, Surrey KT22 7RU. Tel: (0372) 376161.
Press Council
  1 Salisbury Square, London EC4Y 8AE. Tel: 01-353 1248.
St Bride Printing Library
  St Bride Institute, Bride Lane, Fleet Street, London EC4Y 8EE. Tel: 01-353 4660.
Society of Picture Research and Editors (SPReD)
  Box 259, London WC1N 3XX. Tel: 01-404 5011.
Society of Typographic Designers
  17 Rochester Square, Camden Road, London NW1 9SA. Tel: 01-267 4009.
Worshipful Company of Stationers and Newspaper Makers
  Stationers Hall, Ludgate Hill, London EC4M 7DD. Tel: 01-248 2934.

Journals and magazines

British Printer
30 Old Burlington Street, London W1X 2AE. Tel: 01-434 2233.

Campaign
22 Lancaster Gate, London W2 3LY. Tel: 01-402 4200.

Graphics World
7 Brewer Street, Maidstone, Kent ME14 1RU. Tel: (0622) 50882.

Litho Week
Haymarket Publishing Group Ltd, 38-42 Hampton Road, Teddington, Middlesex TW1 OJE. Tel: 01-977 8787.

Magazine Week
Mitre House, 44 Fleet Street, London EC4Y 1BS. Tel: 01-583 3030.

Offset Printing & Reprographics
Maclean Hunter Ltd, 30 Old Burlington Street, London W1X 2AE. Tel: 01-434 2233.

Paper
Benn Publications Ltd, Sovereign Way, Tonbridge, Kent TN9 1RW. Tel: (0372) 364422.

Paper Facts & Figures
Benn Business Information Services Ltd, Sovereign House, Sovereign Way, Tonbridge, Kent TN9 1RW. Tel: (0732) 362666.

Paper Market Digest
Paper Publications Ltd, c/o 14 High Street, Kings Langley, Hertfordshire WD4 9HT. Tel: (09277) 61116.

Print
NGA, 63-67 Bromham Road, Bedford. Tel: (0234) 51521.

Print Buyer
Benn Publications Ltd, Sovereign Way, Tonbridge, Kent TN9 1RW. Tel: (0372) 364422.

Publisher
Conbar House, Mean Lane, Hertford, Hertfordshire SC12 7AS. Tel: (0992) 5834233.

UK Press Gazette
Mitre House, 44 Fleet Street, London EC4Y 1BS. Tel: 01-583 3030.

Training Contacts

There are numerous colleges and companies offering training to those who work in magazines so we have restricted entries to organisations mentioned in the text.

Cardiff University

Centre for Journalism Studies, University College, Cardiff, 69 Park Place, Cardiff, CF1 1SL. Tel: 0222 874786.

Communication, Advertising and Marketing Education Foundation

Abford House, 15 Wilton Road, London SW1 V1NJ. Tel: 01-828 7506.

City University

Graduate Centre for Journalism, St John Street, London EC1V 4PB. Tel: 01-253 4399.

London College of Printing

Department of Journalism, Elephant and Castle, London SE1 6SB. Tel: 01-735 8484.

Newspaper Society

Training Department, Bloomsbury Square, 74-77 Great Russell Street, London WC1B 3DA. Tel: 01-636 7014.

Periodicals Training Council

Imperial House, 15-19 Kingsway, London WC2B 6UN. Tel: 01-836 8798.

Reading College of Art and Design

Department of Graphic Communication, Kings Road, Reading RG1 4HJ. Tel: 0734 583501.

Reed Business Publishing

Quadrant House, The Quadrant, Sutton, Surrey SM2 5AS. Tel: 01-661 3500.

Sources

In addition to information provided by many contacts in the industry, facts and statistics have been used from the following sources:

British Business Press, 800 Business Advertisers, 1986.

Fourth Quarter Figures; Advertising Association, 1988.

Audit Bureau of Circulations Report, 1988.

Manpower and Training in the Periodicals Industry; ICBA Research, 1988.

International Report on Periodical Publishing; International Federation of the Periodical Press, 1988.

Business Ratio Report: Periodical Publishers Industry Sector Analysis, 11th edition; ICC, 1988.

Periodical Magazine Publishing in the 1990s; PIRA, 1988.

Careers in Periodical Publishing; Periodicals Training Council, 1988.

Report for 1987/88; Code of Advertising Practice Committee.

Guide to Good Practice in Controlled Circulation, Subscriptions, Reader Service; Periodicals Training Council.

Magazine and Journal Production, Michael Barnard; Blueprint Publishing, 1986.

Choosing and Using an Advertising Agency; Director Publications, 1985.

Women's Magazines: An Industry Sector Overview; Keynote Publications, 1989.

The Business Press: An Industry Sector Overview; Keynote Publications, 1989.

Consumer Magazines: An Industry Sector Overview; Keynote Publications, 1989.

Glossary of terms

a/w See **artwork**.

A4 European standard paper size (210mmx297mm) commonly used as a magazine format.

AA Author's Alteration See **author's corrections**.

ABC Audit Bureau of Circulation Organisation which prepares audited reports on the circulations of publications.

above the line In marketing, this means advertising costs. Other promotional costs such as public relations activities are termed 'below the line'.

abridgement A shortened version, usually of a book. Hence an **abridged article**.

access The ability to retrieve data from a computer storage medium or peripheral device.

ad Advertisement.

Advertising Association Principal body representing the advertising industry.

adhesive binding Binding style for books and magazines involving the application of a hot-melt adhesive to the roughened or ground back to hold pages and cover together. Also called **perfect binding, cut-back binding, thermoplastic binding**.

agent A publisher's agent is one who acts for the publisher in selling subscriptions.

appraisal System of requiring managers to appraise the performance of their staff at regular intervals, usually with a written record of achievement and objectives.

artist Produces the artwork for the graphic design of a publication's covers and for the illustrations in the publication.

artwork Original illustrative copy or typesetting ready for reproduction at pre-film stage.

author's corrections Corrections made by the author on proofs and changing the original copy, as distinct from **literals** (qv) made by the typesetter.

author's proof Corrected proof sent to the author for approval.

back margin The margin of a magazine nearest the spine.

back number Copy of a previous issue of a periodical.

band strapping Enclosing a stack of magazines with a strong, thin plastic band to secure it. The machine is a **band strapper**.

bar code Symbol representing a unique product code, presented in standardised machine-readable form, and appearing on the outside of a publication for stock control purposes.

below the line In marketing, this means sales promotion costs other than advertising. Advertising costs are called **above the line**.

binding 1. The process of fastening printed sheets together and securing them in a cover. 2. The bound part of a publication, ie cover, stitching, etc.

black and white Single colour black-only originals or reproductions, as distinguished from multi-colour. Sometimes called **mono** or **monochrome**.

bleed Printed matter running off the cut edge of a page. The bleed allowance beyond the **trimmed size** is usually 3mm or $^1/_8$" to ensure a clean cut-off

blow-up To enlarge photographically; or a print so made.

boxing out Sales exercise in which additional, unordered copies of a magazine are sent out to retailers on a **sale or return** (qv) basis. Retailers have individual 'boxes' in wholesalers' offices in which their magazines are placed prior to delivery.

BAIE British Association of Industrial Editors. Association representing editors and employees of **house magazines** (qv).

BPIF British Printing Industries Federation.

BRAD Acronym for **British Rate and Data**. Publication listing all UK publications and their advertising specifications and requirements.

bulk wrapping Wrapping several copies of a periodical, as distinct from individual wrapping.

business-to business Advertising by one business to other businesses who are customers.

camera ready artwork or camera ready copy (CRC) or camera ready paste-up (CRPU) Type-matter or type and line artwork pasted up into position ready for photographing.

caption Text accompanying and describing an illustration.

carrier sheet Sheet of paper, normally the same size as a magazine, on which an address label can be positioned.

casting off Calculating the number of pages a given amount of copy will make when set in a given typeface and size to a given area.

catch line A temporary heading on a manuscript or proof for identification.

centre spread The two facing pages at the centre of a **signature** (qv).

chapel Smallest unit of a journalists' union's departmental or company grouping. **Father of chapel** or **Mother of chapel** is the elected chairperson.

character Letter, figure or symbol of type.

character count Total number of characters and spaces in a piece of copy.

chief sub editor Head of a team of **sub editors** (qv).

circulation The number of copies of one issue of a magazine distributed to buyers.

classified Advertisements for job vacancies, articles for sale, etc, set in columns and sorted by classification.

clean proof A printer's proof in which there are no errors.

coated paper Paper coated with china clay or similar to give a smooth surface suitable for half-tone reproduction.

collate Gather sections of a printed work in the correct sequence for binding. Can be manual or automatic.

colophon A printer's or publisher's identifying symbol, printed on spines and title pages.

colour separation Separating full colour into the four process colours by means of filters, resulting in four sets of film used to make printing plates.

colour swatch A sample of a specified colour.

colour transparency A full colour photographic positive on film.

column inch A newspaper measure of text space: one column wide and one inch deep. Also **column centimetre**.

commission In relation to advertisement sales, commission is a percentage paid to the agent or sales person who makes the sales.

commissioning Ordering articles, pictures or other work from free-lance contributors.

comp 1. To **compose** (qv). 2. A **compositor** (qv). 3. A **comprehensive:** a layout showing everything in position.

compose To make up type into lines and/or pages.

compositor Typesetter who makes up pages.

computer typesetting The use of a computer to store and display typesetting and to perform many other functions such as hyphenation and justification.

condensation A shortened version of a longer work.

consumer magazine Periodical circulated to the general public and dealing with broad areas of interest.

contents page Page of a magazine explaining the contents and where they appear.

copy Material for publication, especially manuscript for typesetting.

copy prep Copy preparation. Putting instructions on manuscript to ensure understanding of requirement by the **compositor** (qv).

copy sales Sales of copies of a magazine as distinct from advertisement sales.

copyfitting Determining the typographical specification to which a manuscript needs to be set in order to fill a given amount of space.

copyright The proprietary right in a work as defined by law.

copywriter A person employed to write the text of advertisements and other promotional materials.

CRC See **camera ready copy**.

credit A printed acknowledgement of the contribution made by a third party to a published product. Typically, copyright owners of illustrations used, artists and photographers receive credits.

crop Cut back part of an illustration to give better effect or achieve better fit.

cross-head A sub-heading ranged centrally over a column.

CTN Confectioner, Tobacconist, Newsagent A generic grouping of traders selling magazines, newspapers and other items.

defamation The issuing of information or views about a person which are libellous and tend to damage that person's reputation.

definition The degree of detail and sharpness in a reproduction.

delivery note A documentary confirmation of the receipt of goods usually signed by the recipient at the time of delivery.

designer In the publishing world, a designer conceives the overall appearance of a printed work. This includes page layout, use of illustrations and typography.

desktop publishing Marketing term describing the concept of technically untrained office personnel producing fully page made-up documents using a custom-made, graphics-orientated micro linked to laser-printer (a **desktop publishing system**).

dimension marks Marks on camera copy indicating area of a reduction or enlargement.

discount Usually the percentage reduction on the retail or list price of a publication offered by the publisher to a wholesaler or retailer.

display ads Advertisements 'displayed' to occupy part or all of a page rather than set in columns.

display matter Typography set and displayed so as to be distinguished from the text, eg headings.

distance learning Learning carried out usually by correspondence course from a training organisation.

distribution The physical delivery of copies of a magazine to wholesalers, retailers and readers.

double page spread See **double spread**.

double spread Print going across two facing pages.

draw program Computer software which enables a designer to create drawings and diagrams on a screen for later output to a laser printer or phototypesetter.

dummy Mock up of a magazine or other piece of printing to indicate specifications.

edit Check, re-arrange and correct data or copy before final presentation.

editing terminal Visual display unit capable of retrieving file and editing the contents prior to processing.

edition All the copies of a printed work from the same set of type or plates.

editorial board Team of experts who form and monitor the editorial policy of a periodical.

editorial work Although strictly it includes the role of commissioning new articles and determining which new contributions to publish, the term is commonly understood to refer to the preparation of manuscripts, illustrations, proofs etc, prior to the manufacture of a publication.

electronic composition Computer-assisted page make-up.

electronic mail Transfer of documents or messages between computers or word processors using direct links, telecommunications or satellites.

electronic publishing The publication and circulation of information in electronic rather than printed form.

EPOS Electronic Point of Sale System for using bar code readers to monitor electronically each copy of an item sold and automatically produce sales and stock statistics.

even pages Left-hand, or verso, pages, with even numbers.

even working Number of pages in a section which will completely fill one sheet of the printing size.

extent Number of pages in an issue of a publication.

face A style of type, ie typeface.

facing pages Pages which face each other in an open book or magazine.

facsimile 1. Exact reproduction of a document or part of it. 2. Machine which copies and transmits documents by telecommunications. Hence **facsimile transmission**.

farm out To place work which might otherwise be done in-house with an outside contractor.

fax Abbreviation for **facsimile transmission**.

feature Substantial article giving background information on a subject.

figure A line illustration referred to in the text of a book.

file A collection of related computer records.

filler advertisement Advertisement used to occupy redundant space rather than booked for insertion.

film make-up Positioning pieces of film ready for platemaking. **Page make-up** is used as the term for pages or **assembly** for **full imposition**.

filmsetting Creating type on to film by means of a photosetting system.

FIPP International Federation of the Periodical Press.

firm sale Method of trading in which the retailer is committed to buying the copies ordered and cannot return unsold items.

first proof The earliest proof used for checking by proof readers.

flat plan Diagrammatic scheme of the pagination of a magazine.

flat wrapping Wrapping a magazine with film or paper without folding it.

FOC Father of Chapel Journalists' union equivalent of shop steward.

folio Page number at the head or foot of a page of text.

foot Bottom of a magazine or page.

fore-edge outer edge of a page, opposite the binding edge.

format 1. The physical specification for a page or a magazine. 2. Frequently occurring set of typographical commands stored as a code on a phototypesetter.

fount A complete set of characters all of the same typeface and point size.

four colour See **four colour process**.

four colour process Colour printing with the three subtractive primary colours (yellow, magenta, cyan) plus black. The colours are separated photographically.

free distribution Term applying to magazines which are free to the recipient.

free sheet Magazine given free to readers.

front end General term for the parts of a photosetting system used before input to a slave typesetting machine, eg keyboard, screens, editing facilities, etc.

front matter The preliminary pages of a publication.

full colour Four colour process.

full-service agency Advertising agency offering full range of services to its clients, including design, media-buying, campaign planning, etc.

ghost writer Someone who writes on behalf of another person who, by agreement, takes credit for the work.

going-to-bed The term used to describe the stage at which a publication is ready for printing and when no further changes can be made.

graphics Pictures and illustrations in printed work.

graphic design The design of matter for publication including typography and layout.

gravure printing Process in which recesses on a cylinder are filled with ink and the surplus removed with a blade. The paper contacts the cylinder and 'lifts' the ink from the recesses. Used for long-run magazines and catalogues.

grid Sheet with ruled lines used to ensure square make-up of photocomposed material.

gross profit The profit left after deducting the cost of sale from sales and other revenues. It is effectively the publisher's profit before taking account of the recovery of **overheads** (qv).

gutter Binding margin of a magazine or space between columns.

h&j Hyphenation and justification.

hack A term, often intended as derogatory, meaning a writer who produces work on demand, in a mechanical fashion and exclusively for the payment offered for the work.

half-tone Illustration created by dots of varying size, resulting in the appearance of 'continuous tone'. Therefore, **half-tone negative** and **half-tone positive**.

hardware Computer term for equipment as distinct from programs.

head Top – or top margin – of a page.

head margin The white space above the first line on a page.

heading See **headline**.

headline A displayed line or lines at the top of a page or piece of text. See also **running headline**.

heat sealing Closing plastic bags by semi-melting techniques.

high density plastic Thin, strong plastic film used for wrapping magazines where weight is critical.

house A conventional term referring to a publishing company.

house advertisement Filler advertisement (qv) for a periodical's own company.

house copies Copies of a magazine for use within the publishing house rather than for sale.

house style See **style of the house**.

house magazine Periodical published internally by a company or other organisation and not usually on general sale to members of the public.

human resources Management of the personnel function within a company.

idle time Time on a machine when it is not in use for production work.

illustrator An artist who illustrates text creatively, usually with drawings.

imposition Arrangement of pages in a sequence which will read consecutively when the printed sheet is folded. Hence **imposition scheme**.

imprint Publisher's and/or printer's identifying text printed in a book or other work.

in-house A term referring to the internal environment of a publishing company. In-house resources, for example, are those a publisher can use without going outside the company.

indicia Formal mailing information or permit printed on an envelope or item to be mailed.

indirect costs See **overheads**.

information retrieval Holding text in an electronic file so that it may be accessed by a computer.

insert Separately prepared printed piece inserted loosely into another publication.

insertion The inclusion of an advertisement in a magazine.

inside front The inside front cover of a magazine.

intellectual property A legal concept which attributes proprietorial rights to the works of the mind and imagination.

ISSN International Standard Serial Number

issue All the copies of a magazine published on one occasion.

JICNARS Joint Industry Committee of the National Readership Survey Organisation which conducts samplings of magazine readership and produces statistics about them.

journal A periodical publication usually devoted to a single subject or a group of closely related subjects.

justification The spacing of words to a predetermined measure, giving 'straight' left and right margins.

key Keyboard text.

key drawing, keyline Outline which positions artwork on a page.

key numbers Numbers on advertisements which identify the source in which they appeared.

keystroke One key depression, often used as a measure of productivity of an operator.

kicker Short line above a headline, set in smaller type.

kill Delete unwanted matter.

landscape Illustration that is wider than it is deep, as distinct from **portrait**.

layout Sketch of a publication, showing the plan to work to.

lead-in The introduction in a piece of setting, often in a bold or different face.

leaf Single sheet, comprising two pages.

learned journal Academic periodical containing research papers.

legend Caption (qv).

libel Publication of information that is false and defamatory.

lineage Classified advertising sold at a rate per line published.

list List of potential customers to be mailed.

literal Mistake introduced in keyboarding, often only affecting one or two characters.

lithography Planographic process in which ink is applied selectively to the plate by chemically treating image areas to accept ink and non-image areas to accept water. Shortened to **litho**.

logotype Company name or product device used in a special design as a trademark. Shortened to **logo**.

London College of Printing (LCP) Major college specialising in training for the print and publishing industries.

long run A high printing number for a job.

lwc Lightweight coated (paper).

machining Printing.

magenta Process red. One of the colours used in four-colour process printing.

mail shot Promotional or publicity literature mailed to potential customers.

mailing house Company which specialises in compiling lists of potential customers and mailing publicity material to them.

make-ready Setting up a printing machine ready to run a specific job.

manuscript Abbreviated to **MS**. Typed or handwritten copy for setting.

margins Areas of white space left around printed matter.

mark-up Instructions on a layout or copy for the compositor to follow when typesetting or making up pages.

marked proof The proof on which the printer's reader has marked corrections.

mass-market The market for **consumer magazines** (qv).

master proof Printer's proof or reader's proof. See also **marked proof**.

masthead Graphic device which displays a magazine's name on the front page.

mechanical data Information about the technical detail necessary to prepare artwork for an advertisement in a magazine.

media Generic term for the various branches of the communications industry, eg magazines, newspapers, television, etc.

media independent Agency restricting its services to buying space in publications on behalf of advertisers.

mini-web Small web offset machine producing 8pp or 16pp A4 colour sections.

misprint Typographical error.

misregister One colour or more printed out of alignment with other colours.

mock-up A layout or rough of artwork. Also called **visual**.

mono See **black and white**.

monotone Illustrative material in one colour.

montage Several images assembled into one piece of artwork.

MS See **manuscript**.

negative Reverse photographic image on film.

net A sum of money not liable to further discount or deductions.

newsprint Paper made from mechanical pulp for the printing of newspapers and some magazines.

new technology Generic term used to describe the use of computers and electronics in publishing systems.

NVQ's National Vocational Qualifications Proposed qualifications relating to specific achievements within a trade or profession.

offprint Part of a book or journal printed separately, eg an article from a journal.

offset Printing which uses an intermediate medium to transfer the image on to paper, eg a rubber blanket wrapped around a cylinder as in offset litho.

offset lithography See **offset**.

opening Facing pages.

original Photograph or drawing to be reproduced.

origination All the processes involved in the reproduction of original material, including make-up, up to plate-making stages and also including typesetting.

out-house Action taking place outside the physical confines of a publishing house.

out of register One or more colours out of alignment with the others in a piece of printing.

outside back The outside back cover of a magazine.

outwork Operations put out to another company for reasons of specialism or capacity.

overheads Costs associated with the fixed liabilities of a business, eg staff and accommodation, as distinct from **variable costs** (qv).

page make-up Assembly of the elements in a page into their final design.

page proof Proof of a page before printing.

pagination Page numbering.

paint program Computer software which enables a designer to create complex graphics on a screen for later output to a laser printer or phototypesetter.

partwork Publication issued in a number of parts which can be purchased separately and which then combine to make up the whole.

pass for press The expression used for a publisher's confirmation that machining of a publication can begin.

paste-up Dummy or artwork comprising all the elements pasted into position.

perfect binding Adhesive binding widely used on magazines. Glue is applied to the roughened back edges of sections to hold them to the cover and each other. Also called **adhesive binding, cut-back binding, thermoplastic binding**.

periodical Publication issued at regular intervals.

photcomposition Typesetting performed by a photosetter.

photocopy 1. Duplicate of a photograph. 2. Duplicate of a document, etc, produced on a copying machine.

photogravure Gravure printing in which the cylinder image is photographically produced.

photosetting See **phototypesetting**.

photostat Trade name for a photocopy.

phototypesetting Setting type on to photographic paper or film. **Phototypesetters** employ various techniques to create the image, with computers assisting in the operation logic.

PIRA The Printing Industries Research Association The national body in the UK which provides its members with information, research facilities and training in the field of printing and publishing technology.

plagiarism Passing off someone else's literary work as your own.

polythene wrapping See **plastic wrapping**.

portfolio Collection of specimens of a designer's or artist's work.

portrait The shape of an image or page with the shorter dimensions at the head and foot.

positive An image on film or paper in which the dark and light values are the same as the original, as distinct from **negative**.

PPA Periodical Publishers Association Representative organisation of magazine publishers in the UK.

pre-press costs All the costs associated with bringing a job ready for press up to but not including printing the first copy. As distinct from **press costs**.

pre-press proofs Proofs made by techniques other than printing.

preprinted Part of a job printed before the main run through on the press.

press costs The costs associated with printing and manufacturing a job from plates onwards. As distinct from **pre-press costs**.

press proof Proof taken from the press after make-ready but before the full run.

Presstream Post office distribution system which offers a discount for magazine mailings in return for various degrees of sorting by publishers.

print A photograph.

print number The number of copies of a publication which a publisher manufactures at one time. Sometimes also called a **print run**.

process colour See **four colour process**.

production Physical printing processes of a magazine or the control functions associated with these.

production editor Member of the editorial staff who liaises on production matters.

promo Promotion. Gaining publicity for a magazine or its activities.

proof A trial printed sheet or copy, made before the production run, for the purpose of checking.

proof-reader's marks Symbols used by a proof-reader in marking corrections on proofs.

proof-reading Checking typeset proofs for accuracy.

PTC Periodicals Training Council The recognised training board for the magazine industry.

publication date A date fixed by the publisher before which no copies of a work may be sold to end users.

publishing house Traditionally, orthodox print-based publishing companies are referred to as 'houses'.

rate card Document issued by a magazine to describe its advertising services and prices.

reader's proof First galley proof used by the printer's reader.

register Positioning of colours accurately to form a composite image.

repro See **reproduction**.

reproduction 1. The quality of printing of a publication. 2. The processes associated with creating artwork in a technical form suitable for printing.

response rate Number of responses to a **mail shot** (qv) expressed as a percentage of the total number mailed.

returns Unsold stocks returned by a newsagent with the publisher's prior agreement.

revise A revised proof for subsequent reading.

rights In a published work, rights are those licences granted to the publisher by the copyright owner of the work enabling the publisher commercially to exploit it, either directly or through the granting of sub-licences to third parties.

ROP Abbreviation for 'Run of Paper'. In magazines or newspapers, material printed as part of the main text.

rotary Printing from plates on cylinders.

rotogravure Gravure printing on a rotary press.

rough A sketch or **layout**.

rough proof Proof for identification rather than reading.

run-around Type set around a picture or other element of design.

running head A title repeated at the top of each page. Also known as **running headline**.

s/s Abbreviation for 'same size' in reproduction specifications.

saddle stitching Binding with wire staples through the middle fold of sheets.

sale or return A trading basis agreed between publisher and wholesaler or retailer whereby unsold stock can be returned for credit after a specified time.

scaling Calculating or marking the enlargement or reduction of an original for reproduction.

scanner Electronic equipment which reads the relative densities of camera-ready copy to make colour separations.

schedule A key task in publishing is to schedule editorial and production work so that issues are put together in a pre-planned manner.

screen The dot formation in **half-tones** (qv).

section A folded sheet forming part of a magazine.

semi-display Advertisements displayed in boxes or laid out as a full or part page within classified advertisement pages.

separation See **colour separation**.

serial rights The subsidiary right in a published work conferring a licence to serialise the work in an agreed manner in a periodical publication such as a magazine or newspaper.

series Advertisements booked to run through several issues of a magazine.

series discount Discount given to advertisers who book ads in **series** (qv).

set To typeset.

sheet fed Printing by separate sheets as distinct from reels.

shoot Photograph.

short run A small print run, usual when a publisher is producing a highly specialised work. Some short run academic titles are produced in runs of just a few hundred copies.

shrink wrap Plastic film wrapping.

signature See **section**.

software Computer programs.

space In advertising, the space offered for sale for advertisements in publications. Hence, **space-selling**.

spec Specification.

special positions Pre-determined positions for advertisements which can be booked within a magazine, eg facing the Contents Page.

spot colour Single additional colour printed in a black work.

stitch To sew with thread or staple with wire as a binding function.

style of the house Typographic and linguistic rules of a publishing house. Also **house style**.

sub 1. Sub editor: journalist who edits copy. 2. Subscription to a magazine or journal.

subscribers Readers who place regular orders for delivery of a magazine by mail.

tails Bottom margins of pages.

take An amount of copy for typesetting allocated to one operator. Part of a newspaper story which has been divided up for speed of setting.

telecommunications Communication over the telephone wire.

terminal Keyboard and/or screen for computer communication or text generation.

titles Magazines.

trade 'The trade' is the term used to describe the wholesale and retail newsagent business.

trade distribution Distribution of magazines through newsagents. See **trade**.

transparency Full-colour photographic positive on transparent film for viewing by transmitted light. Suitable as copy for separation.

trim Cut edges off sheets to square up or reduce size. Hence **trimmed size** is the size after trimming.

TS Abbreviation for typescript.

type area Area occupied by text on a page.

typeface A specifically designated style of type, eg Times or Helvetica.

typesetter Person (or company) who sets type.

typographer Designer of printed material.

typographic errors Abbreviated to **typos**. See **literals**.

uncoated Paper with no coating and therefore not suitable for high quality illustrated work.

unit cost The unit cost of a magazine is the total direct cost of its manufacture divided by the numbers of copies produced for that cost.

unjustified Typesetting with even spacing between words, therefore having a ragged right edge.

unsolicited manuscript An unrequested manuscript sent to a publisher by an author hopeful the publisher will consider taking it on.

update Edit a file by adding current data.

variable costs Costs which vary with the format, extent or run of a magazine.

visual A layout or rough of artwork.

voucher copies Free copies of a magazine sent out to advertisers to show how their ads have appeared.

web A continuous length of paper (ie a roll or reel) as distinct from a sheet.

web offset Reel-fed **offset litho** (qv). Variety of possible configurations from mono to multi-unit, high quality colour presses.

wholesaler An individual or company which buys magazines from publishers for onward sale to retailers.

wire stitching See **saddle-stitching**.

wordprocessor Machine using computer logic to accept, store and retrieve documents for subsequent editing and output in typewriter style.

wp See **wordprocessor**.

wysiwyg What you see is what you get. Acronym used to describe a visual display showing an exact image in typeface and style of a page as it will be output.

Index

www.ingramcontent.com/pod-product-compliance
Ingram Content Group UK Ltd.
Pitfield, Milton Keynes, MK11 3LW, UK
UKHW041839280225
455677UK00010B/246